The Wandering
Uterus

The Wandering Uterus

Politics
and the
Reproductive
Rights
of Women

Cheryl L. Meyer

NEW YORK UNIVERSITY PRESS
New York and London

NEW YORK UNIVERSITY PRESS
New York and London

Copyright © 1997 by New York University

Library of Congress Cataloging-in-Publication Data
Meyer, Cheryl L., 1959–
The wandering uterus : politics and the reproductive rights of
women / Cheryl L. Meyer.
p.   cm.
Includes bibliographical references (p.   ) and index.
ISBN 0-8147-5563-1 (cloth : acid-free paper).—ISBN
0-8147-5562-3 (pbk. : acid-free paper)
1. Human reproductive technology—Social aspects.   2. Human
reproductive technology—Political aspects.   3. Human reproduction—
Social aspects.   4. Human reproduction—Political aspects.
5. Birth control—Political aspects.   6. Sex discrimination against
women.   7. Women's rights.   I. Title.
RG133.5.M48   1997
176—dc20   96-35694
                        CIP

New York University Press books are printed on acid-free paper,
and their binding materials are chosen for strength and durability.

Manufactured in the United States of America

10 9 8 7 6 5 4 3 2 1

To my parents,
Charles Louis and Camilla Kathryn Meyer,
a constant source of support, acceptance, and inspiration

Contents

Acknowledgments

Writing this book has been an adventure. As this adventure came to a close, another began: I learned I was pregnant. This news truly moved the research and work I had completed for this book to another level of meaning and relevance. In the few short months since her birth, my daughter, Rachel, has transformed my life in a way I only dreamed was possible.

Every skill necessary to complete this book was cultivated through the guidance of my parents. They continue to teach their children to respect themselves and others, to appreciate the value of an education, and to demonstrate tenacity in pursuing goals in life. You've done a great job, Mom and Dad.

This book would not have been possible without the help of Debra A. Zendlovitz, M.S.W. Deb painstakingly read every word of this text numerous times and provided a great deal of editorial assistance. More importantly, however, she gave me moral support during neurotic crises and helped celebrate triumphant moments. Deb has provided me with a focus both personally and professionally, fostering my growth in both areas.

Two mentors not only influenced but inspired this book. Professor Morrison Torrey of DePaul University awakened me to the importance of women's issues and, through her course on feminist jurisprudence and her personal convictions, enlightened me and encouraged me to find my own voice. Professor Jane

Rutherford, also of DePaul, through her course and her views on family law, challenged me to think more deeply and analytically. I am indebted to both of these instructors for their indelible impact on my life.

The suggestions, direction, and feedback of Katherine A. Hermes, Ph.D., J.D., also enhanced the depth, accuracy, and scope of the book.

Niko Pfund contributed everything a good editor should: knowledge, editorial suggestions, marketing strategies, attentiveness, and a quick turnaround on everything. However, what has made Niko a *great* editor has been his humor, flexibility, and support, particularly during what I perceived as difficult moments.

The research assistance of Laura Markway, Laurel Bloom, and T. J. Williams was invaluable; they offered technical support when the light was exceedingly dim at the end of the tunnel. I am also grateful to the LEXIS research corporation, particularly Katie Nye, for her understanding, patience, and help.

I also want to thank Northwest Missouri State University for providing financial and personal support for my research. In particular, Jon Hixon, Ph.D., has been enthusiastic and accommodating as both my department chair and friend. Carol J. Claflin, Ph.D., has added valuable editorial tips, research guidance, and pregnancy advice.

Finally, I want to thank all of my readers. I hope this book inspires in you a renewed interest in, and commitment to, the reproductive rights of women.

Introduction: The Wandering Uterus

૨૦

*T*he issues surrounding women's reproduction and reproductive rights have historically been tinged with the devaluation of women. The theory of the wandering uterus is a perfect example. The Greek physician Hippocrates is generally credited with first suggesting that hysteria was the result of a wandering uterus: the uterus, he thought, could detach itself and wander about the body, causing dysfunction by adhering to other organs. For example, the uterus might attach to the heart, causing chest pains, or to the stomach, causing gastrointestinal problems. In turn, this would cause women to become hysterical (evidently men were incapable of becoming hysterical). No one knew for certain how to prevent this from happening, but one cure was to anchor the uterus. This could easily be accomplished through either impregnating the woman or keeping the uterus moist through intercourse so it would not seek out the moisture of other organs.

In the second century Aretaeus suggested that the uterus was attracted to or repulsed by certain smells, causing either a prolapse or "hysterical suffocation," respectively. If the uterus was attracted to a smell, it would distend out of the vagina toward it; if it was repulsed, it would ascend toward other organs. Thus, smells could be used to realign the uterus. If the uterus had prolapsed, the cure was to place a repulsive odor near the vagina; if "hysterical suffocation" had occurred, a pleasant odor should be placed near the vagina. These treatments could be enhanced by placing odors near the vagina and nose simultaneously. So if the uterus had prolapsed, place a pleasant smell near the nose and an unpleasant one near the vagina and the uterus could be cleverly deceived into ascending. Such trickery rested on the assumption that the uterus was, in Aretaeus's words, "an animal within an animal." Galen revised Aretaeus' theory, suggesting that the uterus did not move per se; rather, "abnormal" sexual functioning led to "hysterical suffocation." When the uterus could not function "normally" (for example, in the case of a widow), it poisoned the body through retention of menstrual fluid or old semen. One cure for this malady was to provide a way for the patient to return to a "normal" sex life.

Such theories, directly linking hysteria and emotional stability to uterine functioning and heterosexuality, survived in orthodox medical circles up to the late 1800s and clearly demonstrate the influence of sexism on reproductive rights. No one ventured a parallel theory suggesting that when men become aggressive it is because their testicles break free and relocate to other parts of the body. Men's responses were defined as "normal," and women's responses were pathologized because they were not like men's. Today these notions still exist although they have been reassigned to the hormonal influences related to gynecological functioning: the uterus itself no longer causes mental illness but premenstrual or postpartum hormone fluctuations do.

Moreover, the legal system is fraught with paternalistic notions toward women. Women's reproductive systems and rights have become ensnared in the political agendas of the American Medical Association, the American Psychological Association, insurance companies, pharmaceutical companies, other businesses, legislatures and, of course, politicians at every level. Since abortion is the issue that surfaces most frequently, some people naively believe that society does not meddle with the reproductive freedom of women unless the life of a fetus is at stake. This is far from the case.

In this book a collection of ostensibly unrelated issues are woven into a tale reflecting patriarchal intervention into women's reproductive rights from preconception to postpartum. When each of these issues is examined separately, subtle disparities between the treatment of men and women become apparent. But by viewing them collectively and through an interdisciplinary focus that encompasses law, medicine, and psychology, I will show that these disparities mount up to a broad pattern of social injustice, namely, the control of women by men.

The first two chapters present techniques which are designed to provide women (and couples) more control over their own reproductive choices. Ultimately, these practices have also resulted in health risks to women, discrimination, and many unfulfilled promises. The medical profession and the legislatures have refused to regulate reproductive technologies in any substantial way. As a result, a multibillion-dollar-a-year industry continues to spiral out of control. Semen donors are not routinely screened and limits are not placed on number of donations, thus creating safety concerns and the possibility of satiation of the gene pool. Egg donation, which has been portrayed as a parallel process for women, is a risky, invasive procedure that requires tremendous investment on the part of the egg donor and overall has a relatively low rate of success.

Egg donation would not be worthwhile without the advent of in vitro fertilization and its derivatives. In 1978 the first successful birth from in vitro fertilization showed that it was possible to fertilize eggs outside the fallopian tubes and reimplant the embryo in the uterus. Since then reproductive technologies such as in vitro fertilization and egg donation have become so commonplace that they have become fodder for television sitcoms. Roseanne, a sitcom star who gave birth to a child conceived through in vitro fertilization, facetiously described the process on her television show. "Grace Under Fire," another sitcom, aired an episode in which Grace's best friend asks her to be an egg donor. In vitro fertilization has become old news and has paved the way for numerous other procedures, most of which are notoriously unsuccessful and expensive.

Surrogacy was possible before in vitro fertilization if the surrogate agreed to be inseminated with the semen of a man who would later have custody of the child. In vitro fertilization made it possible to implant an embryo in a surrogate when no genetic tie to the surrogate existed and has also provided physicians with an opportunity to experiment with freezing embryos. The issues of surrogacy and frozen embryos have created unprecedented ethical, legal, and medical dilemmas. The legal profession has not begun to catch up to the medical advances and has been drawn into debates better left to ethicists, such as the question of when life begins. This has created numerous legal situations where no one wins, especially not women. Moreover, although the long-term health consequences of the new reproductive technologies remain unknown, the experimental nature of the procedures and the safety issues are not as well publicized as the purportedly rising rates of infertility. As a result, women (and couples) flock to utilize reproductive technologies, surmising that they are victims of the infertility "epidemic."

While the medical profession has been given virtually a free hand to employ these technologies, women themselves have been increasingly regulated. This seems counterintuitive, given that it is much easier to regulate a profession than individuals. Still, laws which allow women to be punished for behaving in certain ways *while they are pregnant* have been proposed, approved, and implemented. The most notable of these relate to substance abuse during pregnancy and are discussed in chapter 3. In short, the medical profession can create lives, even if that means risking the life and/or health of women, fetuses, or children, but a woman carrying a fetus can be punished for making choices which may affect the health of her fetus.

If women's lives are regulated so that they will not put the fetus at risk, then other potential hazards to the fetus should also be monitored and regulated. Yet, as we shall see in chapter 4, many industries besides the medical profession also go unregulated, even though they may represent threats to the fetus. Why should we regulate women's reproductive lives but neglect to insure overall reproductive health?

Another example of this disparity is abortion. Restrictions over a woman's right to choose limit who can obtain an abortion, when they can obtain it, and where it can be obtained. Abortion methods have also been restricted. RU-486, which has been available in Europe for more than a decade has been kept off the American market by political maneuvering. Women are being denied a well-tested option, only to have it replaced by procedures that are less safe and in some cases even experimental. The politics of abortion and RU-486 are outlined in chapter 5.

Finally, if reproductive rights or reproductive health were really an important issue to policy makers, the appalling statistics presented in chapter 6 would not exist. Cesarean sections and hysterectomies would not be the top two surgeries performed in the United States. In many cases, the procedures place women at great risk for little benefit.

Overall, there is little concern in our society for the health and welfare of the mother or the fetus after conception but much concern over regulating pregnant women. Once genes are safely en route to the next generation, all concern seems to dissipate for the mother or the fetus. All of these issues reinforce the notion that the social, political, and legal focus on women's reproductive rights is driven less by concern for the health of the mother and the fetus than by a societal desire to control women, regardless of the consequences.

This book is intended to be a wide-ranging introduction to issues related to women's reproductive rights and welfare. It is meant to enhance the awareness of those who are beginning to explore these issues, for without awareness there can be no change. Most of the topics touched on here are explored extensively and in greater depth elsewhere, in insightful publications offering sophisticated analyses of subtle nuances and debates that are beyond the scope of this book. This book is not primarily directed at the feminist scholar or at those already immersed in the field of reproductive rights. It is, rather, for all women and men who fight on a daily basis to make informed decisions about their lives.

[1]

Politics and Reproductive Technologies I: Gamete Donation

❧

$\mathcal{R}$osanna and Mauro della Corte were devastated when their only child, Riccardo, was killed in a traffic accident at seventeen. Rosanna said, "If you only knew what darkness there is in this house, without a young boy who filled it with his joy and smile. I desire so much to have another face to caress, to be able to hear somebody call me mother."[1] So the della Cortes decided to adopt a child. However, they were considered too old for adoption. Then Rosanna read an article about Severino Antinori, a gynecologist in Rome, Italy, who could assist Rosanna in becoming pregnant. Antinori fertilized a donor's egg with Mauro's sperm and implanted the embryo in Rosanna's uterus. On 18 July 1994, Rosanna gave birth to a seven-pound, four-ounce son. At sixty-two years old, she is considered the oldest woman in the world to give birth.

Postmenopausal mothers or "Methuselah moms,"[2] as they have been dubbed, have become a focus of debate relating to advancing reproductive technologies. These technologies have placed the "miracle" of birth under the control of mere mortals. While many laud this development, others sound the alarm, prophesying outcomes akin to that which issued from Dr. Frankenstein's laboratory.

Sensationalized accounts of reproductive technologies are widely circulated, and virtually everyone has an opinion regarding the morality, ethics, or legality of their use. Yet rarely do those same individuals discuss the impact on women of the new reproductive technologies. While they have definitely provided women (and men) with more ways to acquire offspring, this does not necessarily translate into greater reproductive choice, rights, or control. The focus of this chapter will be on reproductive technologies relating to gamete (egg or sperm) donation, while the focus of the next chapter will be on in vitro fertilization, including surrogate mothering and cryopreservation (freezing) of embryos.

Alternative Insemination

Alternative insemination (or AI, formerly known as artificial insemination) is the most widely practiced, successful, and notorious of the reproductive technologies. It has even been satirized (generally without much success) by Hollywood, as in Whoopie Goldberg's *Made in America*. However, lumping AI in with the new reproductive technologies is somewhat misleading.

First, AI does not involve much technology. It didn't take the wonders of modern science to figure out the process. Secondly, although medically assisted AI has recently become more popular, probably due to purportedly increasing rates of infertility and the advent of cryopreservation of semen, the possibility of alternative insemination was mentioned in the Talmud,[3] and animal insemination has been practiced for centuries. The first recorded gestation and delivery of a child conceived through alternative insemination occurred in 1790.[4] In fact, legend has it that in 1884, one Dr. William Pancoast anesthetized the wife of an infertile man and, without the permission of the man or his wife, inseminated her with semen from the "most handsome man in his class of medical students."[5] The husband apparently "received the news with great enthusiasm."[6] In short, "by the early 1900's, the practice of DI [donor insemination] was well under way. Twenty-four articles had been written on the subject of DI in the United States by 1938, and a 1941 survey estimated that almost 3,700 inseminations had occurred in the United States."[7] By 1938, the survival of sperm after freezing (cryopreservation) was noted and a successful human pregnancy from frozen sperm was recorded in 1953.[8] What *is* new is the $164–million-a-year "industry" that has developed from the increasing demand for semen and/or semen storage.[9]

It is impossible to calculate the exact number of sperm banks or physicians who perform inseminations or the number of inseminations which occur annually, because there is no federal registry of providers or recipients. Record keeping is often poor, haphazard, or nonexistent, and physicians continue to do improper follow-up. In Canadian fertility clinics, the success rate cannot be established for in vitro fertilization or AI due to poor record keeping.[10] Anecdotal evidence of poor record keeping made national headlines when a New York woman was inseminated with and impregnated by sperm she thought was from her dying husband. In fact, the semen was from an anonymous donor whose race was obviously different from that of the woman and her husband. The woman sued, maintaining that her daughter was subjected to racial prejudice as a result. The case was settled out of court for $400,000.[11] As of 1987, only about half of the physicians regularly performing inseminations in the United States indicated that they had records which would permit them to identify the specific donor for any specific pregnancy.[12]

The best recent estimates regarding insemination practices are from an Office of Technology Assessment (OTA) report, which indicated that approximately 172,000 women underwent medically supervised AI in 1987, resulting in 65,000 births. Most major hospitals claim to have an infertility program involving some aspect of alternative insemination, and an estimated 11,000 physicians perform AI occasionally. There are approximately 150 sperm banks in the United States,[13] supplying semen to physicians, hospitals, or in some cases, private individuals. Sometimes semen from husbands or partners is used. For example, if a man has a low sperm count, semen specimens may be accumulated and frozen, then used during a woman's fertile period. In other cases donor semen is provided.

Donors are paid an average of fifty dollars per ejaculate. If the semen is to be frozen, the ejaculate is generally combined with a preservative (and perhaps other products to prevent the formation of ice crystals) and divided into three or four vials. The vials are cooled, then placed in a liquid nitrogen tank for storage. Sperm can be stored up to ten years, perhaps longer, and still retain effectiveness. Vials sell for an average of $100 to $140 per vial.

Women (and their partners, if they are part of a couple) seeking pregnancy through alternative insemination ordinarily select donors from profiles provided by the sperm bank, hospital, or physician. These profiles may be very cryptic, with little background information about the donor, or may include extensive information, including physical characteristics and family medical history. At least one bank provides an option wherein the patient can select either an anonymous donor or a donor who has signed an "identity-release policy."[14] Donors signing this release policy agree to allow any child conceived by insemination to learn the identity of the donor when the child turns eighteen. This latter option is appealing to many prospective donors as well as recipients.

In a typical program, patients are encouraged to keep track of their menstrual cycles in order to anticipate ovulation. When ovulation does occur, physicians recommend two to three inseminations per cycle, generally twelve to twenty-four hours apart. The semen is thawed (if frozen), drawn into a syringe, and placed near the cervix (or in the uterus if the insemination is intrauterine).

Fresh sperm is more motile and therefore provides a higher rate of conception than frozen sperm. Additionally, using fresh semen can virtually eliminate medical intervention. Quite simply, after the donor ejaculates, the semen is immediately used for insemination. However, choosing frozen semen over fresh has numerous benefits. One is a lower incidence of birth defects.[15] Evidently, healthy sperm have a greater likelihood of surviving the freezing process. In addition, donor semen is sometimes tested and rejected for genetic defects. Another benefit cryopreservation provides is greater flexibility in the AI process. Previously, donors had to be available when ovulation occurred in order to donate. Now, the donor doesn't even have to be present. Nor does a physician.[16] If the health care provider is amenable, and the woman has learned the insemination procedure, the semen specimen can be placed in a portable liquid nitrogen tank or in a cooler of dry ice and insemination can take place at home.

But the most important benefit of cryopreservation is safety. A donor can now be tested for the presence of infectious diseases such as HIV upon donating, and his semen can be quarantined until he is retested six months later. Unfortunately, this is not necessarily standard operating procedure. Physicians still continue to use fresh semen samples and untested donors, disregarding health and safety concerns.

In February 1992, the infamous "love doctor," Cecil Jacobson, was brought to trial for fraud and perjury.[17] Apparently, Jacobson had used his own sperm to inseminate and impregnate female patients while telling them that the semen was obtained from anonymous donors. He reportedly "fathered" seventy-five children through such deception. Jacobson was able to perpetrate such fraud because semen, semen donors, and semen providers are not regulated by any federal agency. Therefore, semen providers, such as sperm banks or private physicians, are not required, *under federal law,* to follow any standards for record keeping. Nor are they required under federal law to screen semen donors in any way, even for infectious diseases like human immunodeficiency virus (HIV) or genetic conditions like Huntington's disease. Even though screening blood donors for the presence of HIV has been federally mandated since 1985, *no such regulations exist for semen donors.* The risk of transmitting infectious disease should have always been a concern when inseminating. Even veterinarians were warned, in 1985, of the risks of diseases transmissible by semen transfer in animals. AIDS has made insemination potentially deadly.

The transmission of HIV through donor semen has been documented in research[18] and anecdotally. The first lawsuit in the world filed by a woman who became HIV-infected through donor semen came to trial in 1991, in British Columbia, Canada.[19] Kobe ter Neuzen was in her thirties, had a career as a psychiatric nurse, and wanted to have a baby. However, she had not met the right partner, and since her proverbial biological clock was ticking, she decided to try insemination. Her attempts began in 1981 and continued through 21 January 1985. She had decided this, her thirty-fifth, would be her final attempt. Unfortunately, on this final attempt, she was inseminated with and infected by HIV-positive semen. The donor had been used to inseminate thirty-five other women over a fourteen-month period. One of those patients, who did not join in the suit, also tested HIV-positive. The physician had been using only fresh semen and had not warned his patients of any risks associated with insemination.

Kobe ter Neuzen sued the physician, Dr. Gerald Korn, and the donor, Eric Kyle, who could not be found for trial. Dr. Korn's screening procedures had consisted of an interview only. He sometimes tested semen for the presence of venereal disease but never screened for HIV. Korn claimed he was unaware at the time (1985, the same year the Red Cross mandated testing of the blood supply) that HIV could be transmitted through donor semen used in insemination. At trial, experts presented conflicting testimony with regard to whether Korn could have been unaware of a link, but the jury found Korn negligent and guilty of breaching warranty of quality goods, awarding ter Neuzen $883,800 in damages. Korn appealed the finding of negligence and the amount of damages awarded, and the appeals court ordered a new trial on these issues.

At least five women in the United States, four women in Australia, and two women in Canada have reported contracting HIV through inseminations. Two of the five American women, Mary Orsak and Cynthia Hallvik, were infected through semen obtained from the same donor.[20] The donor's semen had been used to inseminate fifty-three women, six of whom have not been tested for HIV. Orsak and Hallvik have both brought suits against the physician and clinic involved, the first lawsuits filed in the United States by women infected with HIV through donor semen.

It is difficult to determine how many women have contracted HIV through insemination. Some may not be able to isolate the cause of the infection. Others may not report the cause to the

Center for Disease Control (CDC). It is also difficult to deter-mine how many women have been exposed to HIV through inseminations because record keeping for donors and recipients is often inadequate. At least one woman who was exposed to HIV (but did not contract the virus) filed a lawsuit.[21] Diane Brown was inseminated twice each month from August 1986 through April 1987. The physician, Dr. Sander Shapiro, alter-nated each month between fresh and frozen semen, using fresh for the last two inseminations. After the last insemination, the donor tested positive for HIV. Although Diane Brown tested negative for HIV, she and her husband sued Dr. Shapiro for negligence, medical malpractice, and infliction of emotional dis-tress. The jury found Dr. Shapiro was not negligent, and the verdict was upheld on appeal. It is possible that other women who have been exposed or infected have filed lawsuits but that these suits have not come to the attention of the media and were settled out of court or have not been appealed, which makes them difficult to track.

Many women have risked exposure to HIV from semen that has undergone a controversial "sperm-cleansing" procedure (also referred to as the "swim-up" method). In sperm cleansing, the semen of an HIV-positive man is centrifuged, and the motile sperm which swim to the top are incubated, washed, and col-lected for insemination.[22] Using this method, many HIV-discor-dant couples, where the man is HIV-positive and the woman is not, could theoretically have a healthy child.

Some women have reportedly conceived and given birth to healthy babies using this method, without becoming HIV-posi-tive. In 1989, the University of Milan, reported that fifteen out of twenty-nine women became pregnant through "processed" semen.[23] Ten healthy babies were born, and all continue to test HIV-negative. Conversely, that same year a woman in the United States became HIV-positive after being inseminated with "cleansed" sperm. She did not report engaging in any other high-risk activities. Her physician was fined five thousand dollars and reprimanded by the Virginia State Board of Medicine. The CDC cautions against this technique, but it is not regulated.[24]

In addition to HIV, other sexually transmitted diseases have been transmitted through donor semen. Women have been infected with herpes, hepatitis B, gonorrhea, trichomonas vaginalis, cytomegalovirus (CMV), group B streptococci and chlamydia trachomatis.[25]

State Regulations

Recently, some states have begun to regulate semen providers. Of course, state regulations, by their very nature, are not uniform. Most state statutes contain some provisions regarding donor screening. Some require that the donor be initially tested for HIV infection;[26] others require both this and other tests.[27] However, these statutes do not stipulate restrictions regarding the use of fresh semen, which means that HIV could still be transmitted if the donor's blood had not seroconverted[28] from HIV- to HIV+ at the time of donation. Some states require freezing and quarantining of semen for six months until the donor can be retested for HIV.[29] A few states allow various exemptions from these provisions for spouses or mutually monogamous partners.[30] At least two states require physicians to warn recipients about the risks inherent in the insemination process.[31] Some states require sperm banks operating within the state to be registered with the department of public health. Illinois and Delaware fine banks which are not so registered.[32] Unfortunately, the statutes do not require the registration of private facilities or private practitioners, who can be the worst offenders when it comes to the careless screening of donors.

Violators of state statutes may incur a fine,[33] civil liability,[34] or even criminal liability. For example, in Tennessee it is considered a crime if a person who knows she or he is infected with HIV "transfers, donates, or provides his or her blood, tissue, semen, organs, or other potentially infectious body fluids for transfusion, transplantation, insemination, or other administration to another."[35] These criminal penalties can extend to medical personnel and facilities which fail to test for HIV.[36]

Unfortunately, even where state regulations exist, they are often violated. In 1992, "two staff members at Mount Sinai Medical Center allegedly ran their own unlicensed sperm bank in which they were the only donors, misleading doctors and patients and ignoring good safety practices."[37] One of the staff members involved was a medical resident at the hospital; the other directed the medical school's teaching laboratory. The staff members sold their fresh semen to physicians from October 1989 until January 1992, although using fresh semen violated both medical guidelines and New York state law. Approximately twelve women had been inseminated with the semen. Civil charges, ranging from selling fresh semen to failing to keep proper records, were filed against the staff members, the physicians who used the semen, and the medical center. Mount Sinai claimed the physicians were operating without their knowledge or approval. A health department spokesperson, Peter Slocum, said, "Luckily enough, we don't have any evidence of disease in these cases."[38] This was not an isolated incident, but rather the eighth time New York had shut down a semen bank for disobeying state regulations.

Although some states make valiant efforts to control the hazards of AI through legislation, the existing statutes are inadequate. First, semen is often shipped across state lines. Second, it is virtually impossible to monitor the activities of all the private physicians who might be performing insemination procedures. Third, many women are not informed by their physicians of the risks related to insemination, receive little information about where the semen was obtained, and are unaware of the applicable state regulations. In general, the statutes do not thoroughly address all of the dangers associated with AI, particularly the transmission of HIV. Medical guidelines are more comprehensive.

Medical Guidelines

In the 1987 OTA investigation regarding insemination practices in the United States, 372 physicians' surveys were reported. Of these, only 44 percent tested for the presence of HIV in semen donors, and between 20 percent and 30 percent indicated that they tested for the presence of gonorrhea, syphilis, chlamydia, or hepatitis. All sperm banks surveyed tested for the presence of HIV, but only twelve out of fifteen tested for other sexually transmitted diseases. The physicians demonstrated a similar lack of concern and/or knowledge about genetic defects: 37 percent of them said they would accept a healthy donor with a family history of Huntington's disease, which is transmitted genetically but remains asymptomatic until later in life, while 49 percent said they would reject a healthy donor with a family history of hemophilia even though the donor could not carry the gene for hemophilia.[39] Only thirteen out of fifteen sperm banks tested for genetic defects. Perhaps it was the reporting of these appalling statistics that led the medical profession to attempt to regulate themselves by providing voluntary guidelines.

The first set of formal guidelines were published by the American Fertility Society (AFS) in 1986, although the Public Health Service (PHS) had already, in 1985, recommended testing semen donors' blood for the presence of HIV.[40] By 1988, the Food and Drug Administration (FDA) and the Centers for Disease Control (CDC) had prepared new guidelines, which were endorsed by the AFS, the American Association of Tissue Banks, and the American College of Obstetricians and Gynecologists.[41] Collectively, these associations recommended that physicians no longer use fresh semen for inseminations unless the donor was in a mutually monogamous relationship with the recipient. Instead, semen specimens should be frozen for 180 days and only used if the donor tested negative for HIV antibodies at the end of that period. Additionally, physicians were encouraged to take such precautions as assessing risk factors for HIV and conducting physical examinations of donors. These guidelines remain relatively unchanged, although the AFS has added some provisions, such as those relating to informed consent and limits on donor paternity.[42]

While it is encouraging that the medical profession has finally acknowledged the hazards of donor insemination, the established guidelines are not mandatory, and the penalties or sanctions are minimal. Licenses are seldom revoked nor are stiff fines imposed, so the guidelines continue to be ignored and violated. In the same year that the Mount Sinai employees were charged with operating an unlicensed insemination site, a report prepared by the Canadian Royal Commission on Reproductive Technology was released that reviewed international insemination practices, with a focus on the American scene. It was found that most sperm banks and fertility experts were following guidelines but that some physicians ignored them, continuing, for example, to use fresh semen because they "know and trust their donors."[43]

Dr. Gerald Korn, the physician who is being sued by Kobe ter Neuzen also "knew" his donors. In fact, when he "interviewed" donors, he would not accept semen from what *he* determined were "at risk" populations *for sexually transmitted diseases,* such as homosexual men. Of course, since he did not test for sexually transmitted diseases, he could not actually determine who was infected and apparently labored under the assumption that his donors would not lie to him. Such naive thinking resulted in the transmission of HIV to ter Neuzen and another patient.

A similar example of naivete occurred at a New York sperm bank. In 1993, Idant, one of the most established sperm banks in the United States, violated both state laws and medical guidelines. Idant did not completely screen forty active donors, thirty-one of whom (the "directed donors") had contracted with women slated to be surrogate mothers. The health department determined that of the forty donors, ten had not been tested for HIV, thirty-two were not tested for hepatitis at all, twenty-eight were not completely tested for hepatitis B, twenty-eight were not tested for gonorrhea, and fourteen were not tested for syphilis. Tom Favreau, director of Idant found that "as many as 23 surrogate mothers were inseminated with sperm from the incompletely tested donors."[44] Nevertheless Favreau suggested that the charges leveled against the sperm bank were vindictive, because the problem was being corrected. The reason some tests were not performed, he said, was because he did not think the state's regulations applied to directed donors who were inseminating surrogates to bear their own biological child. Does this imply that directed donors would not knowingly expose a woman to disease but other donors would? Perhaps Favreau believed that a man who would hire a surrogate is such a "nice guy" that he could never carry HIV. Little concern is demonstrated here for the "surrogate" mother or the fetus. The "surrogate" mother is treated less as a patient and more as an incubator. The whole incident is best summed up by Dr. Jeanne Linden, the health department's director of blood and tissue resources: "If nobody caught anything, it is just good luck."[45]

Although the medical profession sincerely hopes to regulate itself through establishing guidelines, it still protects physicians who violate them.[46] For example, when the Canadian Royal Commission on New Reproductive Technologies learned that three physicians were using untested fresh semen, it would not release their names but did agree to identify the provinces where they practiced. Patients and their families were left to wonder whether their own physician had provided "safe" semen specimens, and many undoubtedly suffered emotional distress as they were tested and retested for infectious diseases, especially HIV.

The guidelines not only fail to ensure health and safety but leave too much to the discretion of physicians, especially the selection of would-be parents. No guidelines address discrimination in the provision of services or assert the rights of *all* patients to treatment. This enables physicians to select who should and should not be "allowed" to become parents, and choices may be based on sexual orientation, income, or even race. Dr. Korn, who was already sued for malpractice, made headlines once again in 1993 when he told a lesbian couple that he would not inseminate lesbians. The couple (a doctor and a lawyer), complained to the College of Physicians and Surgeons in British Columbia, who supported Korn's decision. In fact, in 1991, the Royal Commission on New Reproductive Technologies found that being a lesbian was grounds for refusal of insemination services at twenty-eight out of forty-nine Canadian fertility programs.[47] Allowing physicians to determine who is fit to procreate could set a dangerous precedent.[48] However, in 1995, the women won a British Columbia Human Rights Council case against Korn, on the grounds that his actions violated the British Columbia Human Rights Act, which prohibits discrimination based on sexual orientation. They were awarded twenty-five hundred dollars for loss of dignity and nine hundred dollars as reimbursement for the expense of having to seek insemination in another province.

Finally, even though some guidelines attempt to limit the number of children a donor can father, it is impossible to monitor this without some centralized system of record keeping. For example, a donor could reach the paternity limit at one sperm bank (if they have one) and, driven by financial incentives or by narcissistic thoughts of immortality, simply begin donating at another. This not only raises the possibility of satiation of the gene pool but of intermarriage between offspring of the same donor, especially if the recipients of his semen lived relatively close to one another. If this scenario seems unlikely, consider the seventy-five offspring of Cecil Jacobson, all living in the same general region and close enough in age to be potential partners for each other.

Solutions

On the surface, AI appears to offer women greater reproductive choice and control. Women who previously could not have children, because they were single or their partner was infertile or they were lesbians, now can. However, the control and the choices are partly illusory, as they really belong in large measure to the physicians who provide the services. These physicians can choose who becomes a donor and a recipient. They can also determine what tests the donor will receive, what information will be obtained from social and medical interviews, and how those records will be maintained. Additionally, physicians determine what information the recipient receives regarding the results of donor screening. Finally, they may even select the donor for the recipient.

Barbara Raboy, the founder and executive director of the

Sperm Bank of California, which offers a donor identity release option, suggests that such an option is one way to diminish physician control over the AI process.

> When a couple undergoes counseling and is advised not to inform the child, the couple is simultaneously discouraged from asking questions about the donor. As a result of this discouragement, the couple doesn't request donor information. Without the request for donor information, the physician and sperm bank have no incentive to release donor information. Without this incentive, the sperm bank frees itself from the responsibility of long-term donor records maintenance and donor-tracking (most sperm banks still do not conduct follow-up studies of the use of donor semen). Since the physician and/or sperm bank selected the donor for the couple, control over the donor selection process rests with the medical profession and sperm bank. The offering of an identity-release option for sperm donors pierces the reign of control and promotes greater accountability in the practice of DI (donor insemination) and sperm banking.[49]

The current practice of AI may actually curtail choices as well as control. Physicians assume there is no widespread problem and minimize the risks associated with AI. By keeping silent about the hazards they take upon themselves a decision that should rest with the patient: whether the potential benefits of a procedure outweigh its potential risks. A thorough informed consent could allow the patient to make this decision.

Clearly, the best way for patients to gain control and enhance options is to regulate. Mandatory federal regulations, with stiff penalties for violators, may eradicate health risks as well as discriminatory practices. Moreover, the federal government could provide a sealed registry of donors, including such crucial information as medical history and previous paternity. This could virtually eliminate concerns about satiation of the gene pool and intermarriage.

In 1988, then-Senator Al Gore was purportedly writing a bill attempting to establish such a national data bank, but today, eight years later, we still do not have one. In 1991, Representative Ron Wyden of Oregon came closer to regulation when he "introduced a bill that would have forced the embryo laboratories within these fertility clinics to be federally certified. But the Bush administration said it would oppose efforts to require federal intervention into matters that have historically been left to the states." [50] Wyden then wrote a new version of the bill which would have required the Health and Human Services Secretary to design a safe certification program for states to adopt. Wyden also considered "amending the bill so that American Fertility Society (AFS) guidelines on artificial insemination will be considered the 'standard of care' in lawsuits related to the practice." [51] The AFS medical director supported Wyden's initial proposal to certify embryo laboratories, but stated, "We would have serious reservations about supporting any amendments that would appear to regulate the clinical practice of medicine." [52]

Egg Donation

Egg donation is a relatively newer and more complicated procedure than sperm donation. Healthy eggs are removed from a donor's ovaries, fertilized with sperm and placed in a recipient's uterus. The first reported birth from a donated egg occurred in Australia in 1984,[53] while the first reported birth in the United States was in 1988.[54] It is impossible to determine how many egg donation clinics exist in the United States, because, like sperm banks and semen providers, egg donation clinics are not federally regulated. In 1994, *Newsweek* estimated there were three hundred assisted-fertility clinics, generating $2 billion in business a year.[55] Similarly, it is impossible to determine how many children have been born using donor eggs, but a Los Angeles physician and researcher who is considered an authority on the subject estimated that the total was between 750 and 1000.[56] This may well be an underestimate, given the possibility of poor record keeping, especially when eggs are fertilized and cryopreserved as frozen embryos.

Like semen donors, egg donors generally complete a screening process. However, egg donation clinics seem to be more rigorous in their testing of donors. The most rigorous screening of sperm donors generally involves a physical examination, urine analysis, and extensive blood testing for sexually transmitted diseases and genetic defects. Egg donors are not only routinely given these tests but may complete a number of other procedures, including stress treadmill electrocardiography, mammography, chest radiology, oral glucose tolerance tests, fasting serum insulin tests, cervical smear tests, and ultrasounds of the pelvis. Additionally, egg donors are routinely evaluated psychologically through interviews and sometimes testing. Occasionally, even the egg donor's partner receives psychological testing and medical tests for transmittable diseases. If a candidate is deemed acceptable, the medical regimen begins.

The actual medical procedure involved in egg donation usually begins two to four weeks prior to extracting the eggs.[57] First, the donor's natural ovulatory cycle is suppressed through approximately two weeks of daily hormone injections. Then the donor receives daily hormone injections that stimulate the ripening of multiple eggs, otherwise known as "superovulation."[58] Finally, when the eggs have matured enough, a third hormone is injected. Throughout the entire process, donors usually receive numerous ultrasounds of the pelvis to monitor the size of the ovaries and numerous blood tests to monitor hormone levels. These procedures are conducted in order to determine if and when ovulation is about to occur.

Once hormone manipulation is completed, egg retrieval may be accomplished through various potentially dangerous modalities. Initially egg retrieval involved surgical intervention through laparoscopy.[59] At least three women undergoing this procedure have died from general anesthesia complications. Hemorrhage or the rupture of other organs may also occur.

Although surgical intervention is still occasionally used, a more common method of egg retrieval is transabdominal (or transvaginal) ultrasonically directed oocyte recovery, or TUDOR. For this procedure, a general anesthetic is occasionally used, but more often a local will suffice. A needle is then inserted through the vagina or bladder and into the ovary, and the eggs are extracted. An ultrasound is used, primarily to ensure that the bladder is full, a necessary prerequisite to retrieval. The donor must remain relatively immobile during the process to avoid a rupture of the ovaries or other body parts. She may also endure numerous punctures before all the eggs are collected. Although the donors typically return home within a few hours, they usually remain on supplementary hormones and sometimes painkillers until the body returns to normal hormonal functioning.

While the egg donor prepares for egg retrieval, the donor recipient prepares for implantation. Like the donor, the recipient also receives numerous hormones, in order to thicken the endometrium and synchronize her menstrual cycle with that of the donor.

It could be the complexity and invasiveness of the procedure that has led to limited public support and ethical controversies. On the other hand, these controversies may simply represent a double standard regarding reproductive technologies.

Double Standards

Sperm donation creates relatively little controversy anymore and has actually become commonplace. Conversely, egg donation has generated tremendous debate in a short period of time. Numerous books on egg donation have been published, as well as articles in newspapers, journals, and law reviews, while relatively little has been published on sperm donation. Questions and objections arise that have never been broached with regard to sperm donors, suggesting that public attitudes on these issues may be influenced by a double standard.

One controversy focuses on whether women receive payment for donating their eggs. In England, it is against the law to compensate egg donors. In fact, even the AFS has suggested that egg donors should not be compensated except for expenses, time, risk, and inconvenience related to donation. No such qualms about compensatory sperm donors is expressed.

Many facilities maintain that they don't really pay their egg donors per se but merely compensate them for their travel and time.[60] However, even when egg donors are compensated for "time and travel," they are not compensated well. The average compensation is approximately two thousand dollars—a trifling amount, given the time commitment, the invasiveness of the process, and the risks involved. In the selection process alone, egg donors make a much greater time commitment than sperm donors. The selection process for sperm donors may entail a screening that lasts several hours and may require two appointments. Egg donors endure a rigorous screening that involves closer to sixty hours of testing, spanning numerous appointments. If egg donors were paid the minimum rate sperm donors are paid, twenty-five dollars per hour, they would already be earning fifteen hundred dollars from the screening alone. This does not include time involved in the procedure itself or preparation for the procedure. Moreover, sperm donors are not exposed to any risks, while egg donors risk permanent damage from infection or hemorrhaging, which could result in sterility or even death. In addition, hormone injections have been linked to a greater incidence of breast cancer and ovarian cysts, and clomiphene, a commonly prescribed fertility drug, has been linked to ovarian cancer. Hormone manipulation has also produced side effects such as mood swings, weight gain, hot flashes, nausea, breast tenderness, water retention, and ovarian hyperstimulation syndrome (a swelling of the ovaries that calls for immediate medical attention). Finally, sperm donors can and often do continue to donate and make additional money, while egg donors generally only donate once, although it is possible to donate every six months. Given these factors, it is difficult to comprehend why egg donors should not be *better* compensated than sperm donors.

A key issue underlying debate over compensation for egg donors seems to be a concern that payment may make egg donation a baby brokerage business. Once again, this concern never arises with sperm donors, although they have a much greater opportunity to make a profit from gamete donation than women do. Moreover, this concern seems a bit misdirected. After all, it is more likely to be the clinics who exploit the profit potential of the baby-making business and market gametes as a commodity. For example, one Virginia clinic currently advertises in England, offering a large selection of egg donors and no waiting list. This is a direct attempt to take advantage of the market "shortage" of donor eggs in England.[61] Similarly, an English clinic offers free in vitro fertilization (IVF) services to women who agree to donate half their eggs and thereby circumvents English restrictions on compensation.[62] If baby brokerage is truly the concern, then why not insist that egg donation clinics operate on a not-for-profit basis? Or why not regulate advertising rather than limit the payment the donor may receive?

Egg donation costs recipients between ten thousand and twenty thousand dollars per attempt. The fact that everyone involved in the egg donation process, excluding the donor, is amply compensated, is rarely debated. No women have made a fortune, much less a living, from egg donation. Yet numerous critics have argued that women should donate eggs out of altruism. This notion may be derived from the stereotype of women as more altruistic, nurturing, and "life-giving" than men. Perhaps it is really just an extension of the societal notion that women should not be compensated for work, and if they are, they should not be compensated more than men.

Another controversy focuses on the anonymity of donors. Traditionally, sperm donors have remained anonymous, while egg donors were often friends or relatives of the recipient. In fact, originally many clinics required recipients to find their own donors. Now, the movement toward identity-release sperm donors has grown, while egg donors are increasingly encouraged to remain anonymous. Advocates of anonymous egg donation hold that anonymity may prevent egg donors from becoming emotionally invested in the subsequent fate of the egg and somehow attempting to later gain custody or visitation of a child. Once again, no such concern is voiced with regard to semen donors, even though semen donors have contested custody and gained visitation rights of babies born from their donated semen.

Some critics debate whether women should be "allowed" to donate their eggs at all. Rarely does anyone raise the corresponding question with regard to semen donors. Clearly semen donation is not an analog to egg donation. Still, some ethical issues are common to both; for example, the wisdom and legitimacy of interfering in the procreative process. But egg donation seems to cause more distress to the general public and to ethicists than semen donation, perhaps because of the technology involved. This issue may also dissuade potential donors.

Donor Shortage

The first recorded case of an egg donation that resulted in a birth came about rather serendipitously. The donor was in the process of having eggs removed for in vitro fertilization. Five eggs were removed and fertilized, but according to the regulations, only four could be implanted in her uterus. She agreed to donate the fifth, and a child was conceived from it. Initially other egg donors were obtained in similar fashion. Women undergoing sterilization, a hysterectomy, or in vitro fertilization were asked to donate. Unlike semen, unfertilized eggs did not respond well to cryopreservation,[63] so when women were undergoing in vitro fertilization and had extra eggs extracted, they were often amenable to donating them. Generally only a limited amount could be implanted, and the rest would be destroyed. However, with the advent of cryopreservation of embryos (fertilized eggs), women undergoing in vitro fertilization can now preserve their gametes for their own future attempts at in vitro fertilization. Additionally, demand for donor eggs has continued to increase, resulting in an extreme shortage of egg donors. The shortage could also be exacerbated by any number of factors, including the risks of the procedure, its invasiveness, the heavy time commitment and inconvenience entailed, and a lack of widespread knowledge about the need for egg donors. Regardless of the reason, clinics and physicians have suggested inventive alternatives to traditional egg donors.

One recently proposed alternative is to provide egg donor cards, similar to donor cards for vital organs, to all women with viable eggs: women could choose to have their eggs or ovaries removed and donated in the case of their unforeseen demise. Presumably, parents could also consent to donate their daughter's eggs (given that she is under the age of consent) in the event of her sudden death. Therefore, theoretically a child could be born whose genetic mother had died in a car accident when she was too young to even grasp the implications of children or motherhood.

If the idea of donating dead children's eggs to childless couples seems abhorrent, another alternative source of egg donors may rate even higher on the "yuck factor." [64] It is possible that eggs could one day be harvested from the ovaries of aborted female fetuses. [65] Of course, the woman who underwent the abortion, and who would be the genetic grandmother of any child born from the fetus's eggs, would have to consent. However, given the lack of control over the semen donation "industry," it is difficult to imagine how an unregulated egg donation "industry" could be secured against ethically dubious practices. What would stop a physician from harvesting eggs from an aborted fetus without the patient's consent? However, this very real possibility does not appear to generate any concern. Once again, ethicists seem more distressed over the possibility that women may profit from this procedure by establishing "fetal farms," where aborted fetuses would be sold to ovum harvesters. [66] Presumably women would get pregnant and purposely abort (perhaps repeatedly) simply to sell their aborted fetus's eggs. The worry over women profiting from their reproductive capacity extends to absurd proportions.

These options may seem distant possibilities. However, at least one woman in Korea has already given birth to a child who was conceived through the donated gametes of a deceased woman. The medical profession is desperately seeking to increase the supply of egg donors as demand continues to increase.

In part, this demand is due to medical advances which have exponentially increased the number of potential mothers.

"Methuselah Moms"

As debate rages on regarding potential sources of egg donors, new concern has arisen over who should and should not be donor recipients. Severino Antinori's work in Italy has made the possibility of postmenopausal birth renowned and generated tremendous controversy. Although Antinori was not the first physician to successfully impregnate postmenopausal women, his patients are some of the oldest known women to give birth. The concept of "Methuselah moms" has received little support and much criticism. The term itself is catchy and memorable, but also degrading. It is not surprising that many clinics will not accept postmenopausal women as donor recipients. France strictly prohibits assisted conception in postmenopausal women.[67] After the notorious case of Rosanna della Corte, discussed at the beginning of this chapter, Italy also passed regulations regarding the age of donor recipients and other criteria of eligibility (i.e., lesbians and single women are excluded).

Objections to postmenopausal pregnancies often reflect double standards in notions of parenthood. When an older man fathers a child, society seems to revere him as a paragon of masculinity and virility. Yet when older women give birth, concerns abound, ranging from the possibility of the child being orphaned to the capacity of the mother to parent. Even when the father is as old as the mother, it is the mother who is criticized for becoming a parent later in life. This is ironic, given that men have a shorter life expectancy than women and an older father will therefore be more likely to die before his child grows up than will an older mother. Furthermore, older mothers tend to secure extensive support systems for their children and are generally affluent enough to insure that they are provided for in the case of maternal illness or death. Moreover, younger women who are terminally ill or who live or work in high-risk situations are not prevented from having a child, despite the risk of the child being left motherless.

Along these same lines, critics have argued that women of grandparenting age should not be raising children. Yet the number of grandparents parenting grandchildren is rising steadily, as the cost of day care increases and the availability of quality centers decreases. In fact, interaction between children and the elderly is often intentionally arranged, to the mutual benefit of both groups.

Many opponents also claim that older women are simply too frail to go through the trauma of birth.[68] However, embryo recipients are always screened for ill health, and there is little evidence that middle-aged mothers are any more "at risk," in general, than young ones.

Finally, some hold that postmenopausal women who become pregnant are utilizing valuable resources that could benefit a younger mother.[69] How can *anyone* assess benefit, or happiness, or quality of life? It is just as easy to argue that postmenopausal women benefit more from motherhood than do younger women, and make better mothers to boot. They can often afford advantages and luxuries for their children that younger mothers cannot. In addition, their lives are often organized in a way that permits them to spend much more time with the child than a younger mother could. Ultimately, who knows what makes a good parent? Apparently, members of the medical profession believe they know.

Discriminatory Practices

As egg donation becomes more prevalent, catalogs with egg donor profiles are often available to prospective recipients. Like information in sperm donor catalogs, these profiles may cover health, age, race, interests, hobbies, occupation, features, educational level, and family medical history. Prospective recipients can generally select a donor based on whatever criteria are relevant to them. Physicians encourage couples to select a donor whose features will be similar to their own, particularly to the gestational mother's. In fact, before catalogs were available, physicians usually attempted to "match" donors and recipients, provided there were enough donors to allow for selection. Presumably "matching" facilitates adaption by the parents and the child to the absence of a genetic link with the gestational mother and may enable the child to "pass" as the gestational mother's genetic offspring. In the past, adoption agencies regularly encouraged "matching" of this sort, and some still do.

"Matching" is a disconcerting and dangerous concept. It suggests to parents that they may be able to forgo telling children about their genetic background. Moreover it hints at notions of racial purity. Recently the actual racism inherent in the "matching" policy was highlighted when, in separate incidents, two African-American women chose Caucasian egg donors. Their selections made *international* headlines. One woman was married to a Caucasian man; the other woman's husband was of mixed race.

In at least one of these instances, African-American egg donors simply were not available. African-American and Asian egg donors are almost always in short supply, due to a number of possible factors, including less intensive recruiting of minority egg donors. "Ideal" Caucasian donors are actively recruited: "The blond, blue-eyed former college athlete, who is studying to be a surgeon, was welcomed as an answer to a prayer by the hopeful egg recipient. . . . She was paid considerably more for her time then the $350 to $500 recommended by the American Infertility [sic] Society in its guidelines to clinics."[70] Another clinic's donor coordinator, who also had an "ideal" blonde-haired, green-eyed donor, explained, "I wish I had about 20 clones of her in different hair colors."[71] She did not, however, say that she wanted any "clones" with different skin colors.

Some donors are routinely screened out of the process because of their sexual orientation. For example, one clinic refuses to accept lesbian donors because of the possible hereditary component in homosexuality.[72] The logic here, apparently, is that it is better not to have a child than to have a gay one.

These discriminatory practices extend to recipients. Most recipients are Caucasian, upper-income couples. Although upper-income minority couples may seek egg donors, they may become discouraged by the lack of "matching" donors. The screening process for recipients, which is left to the discretion of the clinics and physicians, may also discourage members of ethnic/racial minority groups, as well as single women, lesbians, or anyone else deemed "inappropriate" for parenthood. Egg donation has become a process wherein infertile Caucasian couples procreate while other infertile couples or individuals continue to seek alternatives. This is particularly unfortunate given the increased rates of infertility among people from minority groups. Minority donors are not recruited; minority recipients cannot find "matching" gametes; and when minority recipients "choose" Caucasian donors, they are scrutinized and criticized. For example, when one black woman attempted to obtain eggs from a Caucasian donor, the clinic conferred first with the Human Fertilisation and Embryology Authority before they would proceed. This licensing bureau did not object, most likely because there were no minority donors available. It is unclear what the board would have ruled if eggs from a black donor were available but the couple simply preferred a Caucasian donor. In Italy, such an instance provoked protest from the public and the medical community.[73]

Procreation should be a fundamental right, available to everyone. Yet decisions regarding recipients are left to physicians and, in some countries, legislators. Some recipients are deemed unacceptable because of their age. Others are indirectly discouraged because of their race. Still others are denied access because of their income, marital status, or sexual orientation. In the past, when sperm banks and physicians deemed some women "inappropriate" for parenthood, the women circumvented such discrimination by establishing their own facilities. But egg donation raises concerns that might make it difficult to go this route.

Risks to Women and Their Children

A number of women's issues come to the fore in gamete donation. First and foremost is concern for women's health. In gamete donation it is always the woman who is at risk. The semen donor is in no danger, while the semen recipient often risks the transmission of sexually transmitted or other infectious diseases from semen not tested adequately or not frozen and/or quarantined. It is also the woman who is at risk in egg donation. Most donors experience some side effects from the procedure, sometimes serious ones. The recipient risks complications from hormone manipulation and implantation. Complications can arise in any phase of the process and can lead to temporary or permanent damage. These risks are not always clear to either the donor or the recipient.

The children created by these reproductive technologies also face certain hazards. For example, after "successful" infertility treatment, Helen Pusey became pregnant with quadruplets. She was not cautioned regarding the risks of a multiple pregnancy to either herself or the fetuses. Two of the children died shortly after birth. Both of the surviving children have a multitude of physical problems, and one has severe cerebral palsy. "Doctors do tend to think they are God," Pusey remarks. "They think that they are the experts and they know. But at the end of the day they practice their medical technology but we are left to live with the results." [74] Although the burden is shared by the family, it is generally the woman who will bear the brunt of reproductive mishaps, psychologically and physically.

Most medical innovations begin with animal experimentation and go on to clinical trials with humans. Egg donation began with animals, but unlike most medical research, did not proceed to a controlled study with human participants informed of the experimental nature of the treatment. Virtually on the spur of the moment, the technique was attempted on a woman, succeeded, and became widely available as a new reproductive technology without extensive trials or testing. In essence, women who are currently undergoing egg donation and other reproductive interventions, such as sperm cleansing, *are* the experimental phase of the project. They are "living laboratories," [75] as they have often been throughout the history of obstetrics and gynecology. Marion Sims, renowned as the "father of gynecology," became obsessed with finding a cure for vesicovaginal fistulas, ruptures of the vagina often caused by an instrument used during labor (i.e., forceps). [76] Sims obtained slave women and performed repeated, painful operations on them, without anesthesia, in order to find a way to close the fistula. One woman was operated on over thirty times. Yet Sims believed "that it was his duty as a physician . . . to enable his patients to have as many children as possible." [77]

Given the rigorous regulatory control maintained over the

testing and development of other medical innovations, such as pharmaceuticals, the laissez-faire approach to reproductive technologies is incongruous. Typically, before a prescription drug is approved by the Food and Drug Administration and goes on the market, it must undergo extensive testing for safety (albeit often by the manufacturer). Yet egg donation, an invasive and hazardous procedure, encounters few, if any, governmental roadblocks or safeguards. This certainly cannot be attributed to a general reluctance on the part of the government to meddle with the fundamental right to procreate. Governmental intervention into abortion and contraception choices clearly refutes this notion. It is unclear why the government intervenes in reproductive freedom when the consequences of intervention can be detrimental to women but refuses to intervene when the consequences can benefit them.

Despite health concerns, reproductive technologies are lauded for enhancing women's reproductive control.

> In the next few years the rapid development of new fertility techniques could give women an unprecedented control over their bodies. . . . Imagine your recently married daughter has just been killed in a car accident. You discover that she carried a donor card allowing her ovarian tissue to be transplanted into an infertile woman. Although she was dead, the resulting child would be genetically hers, but you would never see your grand-child.[78]

How does the deceased woman have more reproductive control over her body? If anything, she has lost control. At best, reproductive technologies increase the options available to *some* infertile women. The control over who can and cannot become mothers with the aid of reproductive technology lies with the medical profession, a patriarchal system.

Arguably, reproductive technologies have *diminished* women's control over mothering, particularly with the advent of egg donation. First, the invasiveness of the procedure and its dependence on medical personnel make many women *feel* that they have lost control over their bodies. Certainly hormone manipulation *does* result in a lack of control over their bodies. In addition, physicians control who can be mothers through selective dissemination of information about the process and the selection of "appropriate" egg donors and recipients. Finally, if egg donation follows the same pattern as surrogacy and other reproductive technologies, some women would argue that it will become just another way to preempt women's reproductive choices: "Men have always been concerned with controlling women's fertility and the 'products' of that fertility. That control has ranged from laws which circumscribe women's access to contraception and abortion to religious and political controls which set the appropriate rates of reproduction for women."[79]

The whole issue of reproductive technologies presents a conflict for many women. Some women, for example, who favor reproductive technology in one context (such as abortion), oppose it in another, even though, offhand, it would appear that reproductive technologies are, in their general tendency, "prochoice." Prochoice women often perceive the technologies as a way to strap women into compulsory motherhood. Now there is no excuse for childlessness: women without male partners, women with fertility problems, women past childbearing age— all can become mothers (or can at least make a more intensive effort to become mothers). The new technologies, from this point of view, represent a threat to women's psychological and physical health as well as a means to undermine their control of their bodies. On the other hand, prolife (antichoice) women, who often emphasize the importance of the family, frequently oppose the technologies as artificial and insulting to the sanctity of marriage. Regardless of one's stance, reproductive technologies do not necessarily represent progress.

Regulation

If the regulation of semen donation in the United States is weak, the regulation of egg donation is virtually nonexistent. In France medically assisted procreation is only permitted for couples of childbearing age who are infertile or may pass on an incurable disease. Additionally, egg donors must have had a child previously and must be in a heterosexual relationship. Recipients can only be couples who have lived together at least two years. All parties must agree in writing to the procedure. Finally, embryo donations must be authorized in writing by both biological parents and have judicial approval as well.[80]

In England, the Human Fertilisation and Embryo Act of 1990 requires donor identities to be kept confidential, with criminal penalties for disclosure. The act also established the Human Fertilisation and Embryology Authority, which registers sperm and egg donors so that potential offspring do not intermarry. The authority can also provide basic details of the donor's characteristics to offspring. In addition, the act stipulates that sperm donors can be paid but that egg donors can only be compensated minimally, to cover expenses, although sterilization can be offered for free if women undergoing the procedure agree to egg donation. In general, the maximum number of children allotted per donor is ten, and donors are not permitted to learn the outcome of their donations.

In the United States, aside from the law in Louisiana which bans compensation and a few statutes related to custody, *no* laws regulate *any* aspect of the egg donation process.

Beyond Gamete Donation

Gamete donation is only one component of the new reproductive technologies. Prior to IVF, egg donation was pointless, and it is IVF that has created the possibility of full surrogate mothering, wherein the surrogate has no biological connection to the child. Finally, IVF has afforded infertile couples an opportunity to fertilize an egg and cryopreserve the embryo for future implantation. As we shall see in the following chapter, society is still struggling to comprehend the complexities and consequences of these developments.

[2]

Poitics and
Reproductive Technologies II:
The Legacy of IVF

෴

$\mathcal{U}$nrelentingly the media report spiraling rates of infertility. Illusions of rising infertility rates represent part of the backlash against American women for choosing careers over family or careers in addition to family:[1] infertility is their penance. Perhaps now, women will learn, once and for all, that their place is in the home. Divine intervention has doled out consequences for women venturing out on careers of their own.

These purportedly rising rates of infertility have met with almost frenetic response from prospective parents. In part this may be due to increased social and political emphasis on the family, and in part to erroneous propaganda suggesting that adoption is virtually impossible since the legalization of abortion.

The Infertility "Epidemic"

Media estimates of the number of American couples who suffer from infertility vary, but generally average between 10 and 20 percent. Estimates vary because there is no set definition of infertility. In actuality the rate has probably held steady or declined over the last three decades, but the definition has changed, making it *appear* that infertility rates are on the increase.[2] In general, the variable component in these definitions is the length of time that must pass without conception before a couple is considered infertile. Prior to 1975, a couple would not be considered infertile unless they had failed to conceive after five years of unprotected intercourse.[3] In 1975, the World Health Organization (WHO) shortened this time period to twenty-four months, while in 1988, the Office of Technology Assessment (OTA) in the United States suggested twelve months was sufficient.[4] But some serious objections have been lodged against these new and less stringent criteria.

When the definition of 12 months of unprotected intercourse is used, only 16% to 21% of couples meeting this definition actually remain infertile throughout their lives. Indeed, several studies suggest that about 30% of couples take more than a year to conceive at some time during their reproductive lives.

A reassessment of data from the World Fertility Survey and other studies does not substantiate a core rate of infertility of 10% to 20%. A survey in the United States reported that 8.5% of married couples with the wife aged 15 to 44 years (n = 8,450) were infertile, an estimate that is undoubtedly too high as an indicator of actual lifetime infertility, as the OTA definition of infertility was used. Only 3.8% of that sample had *never* given birth, whereas 4.7% had one or more births before the onset of infertility. These figures obtained in 1988 were unchanged from a previous survey conducted in 1982.[5]

Moreover, frequency of intercourse is rarely assessed. When it is, we see that the actual rate of infertility drops even lower as frequency of intercourse increases.[6] In short, although 8 percent of couples may experience difficulty conceiving, most eventually conceive.[7]

But as reports of a burgeoning infertility epidemic escalated, the medical profession investigated solutions. Overall, the techniques developed did not focus on prevention or treatment of infertility but rather on ways to circumvent the natural route to conception. The most consequential and pivotal of these techniques was in vitro fertilization.

In Vitro Fertilization

Louise Brown, the first "test-tube" baby, has reached child-bearing age. Her birth mesmerized the world in 1978: a child could now be conceived outside a woman's body (i.e., in vitro). From 1978 to 1991 approximately sixty-five thousand babies were born from IVF worldwide, fifteen thousand in the United States.[8] Today there are more than three hundred in vitro centers, and the procedure is performed over twenty-seven thousand times per year, in the United States alone.

The technique which led to the conception of Louise Brown has become standard IVF process. First, eggs are removed from the biological mother and placed in a "test tube" or more accurately, in a culture medium such as a petri dish. Semen from the biological mother's partner (or a donor) is also placed in the culture medium in an attempt to fertilize the eggs. If fertilization occurs, some or all of the fertilized eggs (zygotes) are placed in the biological mother's uterus, usually within twenty-four to forty-eight hours.[9]

In an adaptation of the IVF procedure called co-culturing,[10] eggs fertilized in vitro are placed in an "artificial womb." Technically the "womb" is a tube containing endometrial tissue that purportedly simulates the fallopian tubes. After two days, any fertilized eggs are transferred to the woman's uterus. This procedure is particularly useful for women with blocked fallopian tubes, since the tubes are bypassed. In a variant called introvaginal culturing,[11] the fertilized eggs are deposited in a tube that is hermetically sealed and placed in the prospective mother's vagina for approximately forty-eight hours. After that "incubation period" the tube is removed, and selected embryos are placed into the mother's uterus. Again, this technique is primarily designed to assist infertile females. Often a third party, such as a "surrogate mother" or egg donor, is involved in the process when the female is the source of the couple's infertility.

IVF Techniques to Overcome Male Infertility

In approximately half of infertile couples, males contribute to or are the source of a couple's infertility.[12] Several procedures have been designed that assist in overcoming male infertility. These techniques are particularly useful for men with low sperm counts or immotile sperm. One of the best-known derivatives of IVF is a process called ZIFT (zygote intrafallopian transfer). The only difference between IVF and ZIFT is the placement of the zygote. In ZIFT, the zygote is placed in the fallopian tube instead of the uterus. In a similar procedure called gamete intrafallopian transfer (GIFT), eggs are extracted from the biological mother's ovaries, mixed with semen in a culture medium, and then placed in the fallopian tubes to allow fertilization to take place "naturally." Generally, the same instrument used to "harvest" the eggs, a laparoscope, is used to place the fertilized egg (ZIFT) or the sperm and egg (GIFT) into the fallopian tubes. A surgical incision is usually made in the abdomen (or sometimes the vaginal wall) to enable the laparoscope to reach the ovaries or fallopian tubes.

One of the newest techniques for surmounting male infertility is called intracytoplasmic sperm injection (ICSI). In ICSI, IVF procedures are followed, except that, instead of combining the sperm and eggs in a culture medium and allowing fertilization to occur, single sperm are directly injected into the cytoplasm of individual eggs. The sperm is injected through a tiny needle while the egg is held in place by suction. The first birth from ICSI in the United States occurred in 1993. ICSI is a modification of subzonal insemination (SUZI), a technique developed in the 1980s. In SUZI, three to five sperm are injected into the space between the egg and its protective barrier, the zona pellucida. (The zona pellucida forms naturally around the egg when ovulation occurs, and the sperm must penetrate it in order to fertilize the egg.) In a variation of this procedure termed partial zona dissection, acid is used to "drill" a hole in the zona pellucida; then the egg is combined with thousands of sperm, in the hope that one will succeed in entering it.

It is significant that these new methods compensate for men's infertility through invasive procedures performed on *women*. High-intervention techniques like ZIFT, GIFT, SUZI, or ICSI, all of which involve hormone manipulation, egg extraction, and surgery, carry even more risks for women than the relatively low-intervention techniques of AI.

Recent Innovations in the IVF Procedure

Originally, IVF did not involve direct manipulation of the egg and sperm. Although eggs and sperm were "harvested," penetration of the sperm by the egg occurred "naturally." However, with ICSI and SUZI, physicians can intervene in the actual process of fertilization. Such direct action on the sperm or the egg is termed micromanipulation. In essence, ICSI is "assisted" penetration. In a new procedure known as "assisted hatching," the zygote is micromanipulated.

Once a sperm has penetrated the zona pellucida, it hardens to prevent another sperm from penetrating and attempting to fertilize the already fertilized egg. The zygote begins to divide, and when it has divided into sixty-four cells, the zona pellucida or "shell" begins to "crack." This allows the zygote to make a "connection" with and attach to the lining of the uterus (endometrium). If the shell does not "crack" and/or this attachment cannot be made, the fertilized egg is expelled.

In "assisted hatching," developed by researchers at Cornell in 1992,[13] acid is dripped on the zona pellucida until a hole develops, thereby "cracking" the "shell," presumably without harming the fertilized egg. This procedure must be conducted with precision to ensure that the fertilized egg is not destroyed. "Assisted hatching" is performed after the fertilized egg has divided into eight cells. After completion of the procedure, the fertilized eggs are placed in the uterus.

In 1993, another researcher developed a natural cycle variation of IVF.[14] In this method, hormone manipulation is omitted from the IVF process. Instead, the woman's natural menstrual cycle is monitored. At ovulation the mature egg or eggs are retrieved. Although fewer eggs are harvested by this method, their quality is thought to be enhanced. After all, they are produced "naturally."

How Successful?

As with infertility estimates, estimates regarding the success of IVF vary, largely due to definitional differences. Success could be measured by the rate of impregnation, the number of births, or the "take-home" baby rate. Lacking federal standards to serve as guidelines, clinics were initially free to choose how to represent their success, with predictable results. In 1990, the AFS discussed the need to centralize standards for the accumulation and publication of success rates.

If the actual healthy "take-home" baby rate is the standard, the results of IVF are not promising. Worldwide success averages between 8 and 16 percent; more depressing, *failure* rates are 84 to 92 percent per attempt. Failure rates increase with each subsequent attempt at IVF. The success rates for variations of IVF, such as GIFT and ZIFT, are slightly higher, with ICSI providers boasting pregnancy rates of 20 to 25 percent.[15] However, it is impossible to determine if babies born from any of these techniques had or developed congenital or developmental defects or abnormalities. Moreover, these rates may be deceptive, as they are based on relatively healthy parents; if parents with health risks (particularly mothers) were not screened out of the process, the success rate might decline significantly. It is also possible to manipulate success rates in other ways. For example, by implanting a greater number of embryos into the woman, the likelihood of "success" increases, albeit at the expense of health risks to the mother and potential children.

Costs

The actual monetary costs of IVF vary according to the clinic, the procedures used, and the number of attempts. A single cycle of treatment costs an average of eight thousand dollars.[16] However, most couples are not successful on their first attempt. Researchers estimate the average cost of a "take-home" baby from IVF at a whopping seventy-two thousand dollars.[17] If the couple chooses to use the ICSI procedure, the cost will increase by an average of one thousand to three thousand dollars. Other "extras," such as the need for an egg donor or "assisted hatching," can add thousands to the overall cost of the process. Prior to treatment many couples spend thousands on fertility assessment, testing, and drugs.

One factor that inflates the overall cost of IVF is actually a byproduct of the process: multiple pregnancies. Generally, multiple eggs are extracted during IVF procedures (as well as during egg donation). Once those eggs are fertilized, physicians attempt to implant many of them back into the uterus, so that at least one successful pregnancy will result. The number implanted usually increases with the age of the woman, presumably because physicians believe it will improve the possibility of pregnancy, although research does not entirely support this assumption.

Multiple births may result in a number of complications, including miscarriages, low birth weights, premature births, and cesarean sections:

> Of triplets and quadruplets born after IVF, 64.1% and 75%, respectively, required admission to intensive care, often for weeks. Multiple pregnancy also has considerable social, economic and psychological impact on parents. Prematurity after assisted conception was associated with a perinatal mortality rate of 27.2 per 1000, three times the United Kingdom average for births after natural conception. The increased mortality was almost entirely due to multiple pregnancy.[18]

Comparable statistics are difficult to obtain in the United States because of lack of research, lack of regulation, and lack of follow-up. Some obstetricians and pediatricians do not even learn of the circumstances of conception, as patients are sometimes reluctant to disclose this information.

Some clinics voluntarily limit the number of eggs that can be returned to the uterus to three in order to reduce multiple pregnancies. The British Voluntary Licensing Association (VLA) has limited to three the number of fertilized eggs that can be returned to the uterus on any one occasion. However, Ian Craft, a prominent fertility specialist in England, did not comply with these guidelines, and the only penalty was a one-year suspension of his license.[19] Craft continued to practice, without further sanction, during the year he was not licensed.

Since practitioners in the United States are left to set their own limits on the number of fertilized eggs that can be implanted, it is not uncommon for the patient to end up carrying four or more pregnancies. For example, in a Chicago clinic in 1992, Linda Osborn, then thirty-seven, was implanted with nine embryos, which resulted in five pregnancies.[20] As the number of fetuses increase, so do the risks to both them and the mothers. Consequently, physicians and prospective parents are faced with two choices: either continue the pregnancies and risk the health of the mother and the potential children or selectively abort some of the fetuses. Some couples may be philosophically, religiously, or morally opposed to abortion of any sort. To those who have just invested an incredible amount of time, resources, emotions, and money to achieve these pregnancies, the idea of aborting their "investment" is seldom appealing. Even if the couple can be convinced that selective abortion is in the best interest of all concerned, who selects which pregnancies are to be terminated? Physicians sometimes suggest aborting the least healthy and most accessible fetuses, but this invests physicians with tremendous discretion and control: it is they who decide which fetuses are least healthy and most accessible. How do they decide this when dealing with microscopic beings? Size? Gender?

On the advice of their physician (the same one who implanted the nine embryos), Linda and Jim Osborn agreed to selectively abort three of the five fetuses she was carrying. The physician inserted a needle into the hearts of three of the fetuses, thus terminating their existence. The aborted fetuses were then absorbed into Linda's body. Later she gave birth to healthy twins. One oft-overlooked aspect of such a decision is the psychological impact it will have on the surviving children, if and when they are informed of the unusual circumstances of their gestation and the sacrificial elimination of their siblings.

In addition to the monetary costs and ethical dilemmas related to multiple births, both mother and children face other risks. In general, none of the reproductive technologies present any serious risks to the father.

Risks to the Baby

In January 1994, an English researcher found that children conceived through IVF weighed less at birth and were more likely to be born prematurely than babies conceived naturally.[21] One month later, researchers in Australia reported that they found little difference between babies conceived through IVF and babies conceived naturally.[22] In fact, they indicated that children of IVF had somewhat better social skills. Then, in June 1994, French researchers reported a "higher than average rate of serious deformities" among children of IVF.[23] Other researchers too have reported a greater incidence of anomalies among children conceived through the new reproductive technologies. However, it is not clear whether these anomalies result from the procedures themselves, from the fact that they are often performed on women who (because of age or gynecological problems) offer less than ideal uterine environments, or from multiple pregnancies. Alarmingly few studies have been conducted in the United States. The current patients (and their offspring) are truly "living laboratories."

One thing is certain: to date there is no conclusive research— in fact, there is little research at all—on the long-term effects of IVF (and IVF derivatives) on children. The potential physical, social, and psychological effects are impossible to fathom at this point. The pathogenic consequences of past reproductive interventions, such as the use of diethylstilbestrol (DES) in the 1950s to prevent miscarriage, did not clearly emerge for at least a generation.[24]

Perhaps most alarming is the fact that the newer reproductive technologies (particularly those that involve micromanipulation) circumvent the process of natural selection. Natural selection tends to prevent defective sperm from reaching or penetrating the egg and to destroy defective eggs before they can be fertilized. Reproductive technologies interfere with this process. For example, in ICSI, sperm unable to penetrate the egg are injected directly into it. But if sperm cannot penetrate the egg on their own, perhaps they, or the egg, or both, are defective. If so, enabling sperm to penetrate the egg may result in an embryo with genetic defects or weaknesses.

Micromanipulation also circumvents a second natural selection process. If a fertilized egg is defective, it often spontaneously aborts. However, with "assisted hatching," a fertilized egg that would once have been cast off as not viable may now attach to the wall of the uterus and develop. In addition, the effect of weakening the zona pellucida on the fertilized egg is unknown. While IVF *facilitates* conception (in cases, for example, where it has been blocked by anatomical problems in the mother or father), micromanipulation *forces* it, providing little or no opportunity for natural selection to occur.

The potential consequences of these interventions are disturbing, and to counter them, researchers have developed their own methods of natural selection. Now, with embryo screening, also known as preimplantation diagnosis, it is possible to test an embryo for genetic defects prior to implanting it in the mother. For years amniocentesis and chorionic villi sampling have been used to screen fetuses of potentially high-risk mothers for genetic defects. If these tests revealed genetic defects, the patient(s) were given the option of terminating the pregnancy. With IVF, patients can make this decision before implantation. Theoretically, embryos could eventually be screened for genetic diseases or deformities and other "undesirable characteristics." For example, one would no longer have to resort to abortion or infanticide to get rid of unwanted female offspring: they could simply be "screened" out in vitro. Imagine the possibilities if genes for homosexuality and heterosexuality could be pinpointed—a real and frightening prospect given the recent discovery of what may be a "gay gene."

Other Risks to the Potential Mother

The same risks inherent in egg donation are present in IVF, since the same process is involved. Hormone manipulation and the extraction of eggs can result in numerous complications for women. Both procedures are more likely to result in an ectopic (tubal) pregnancy, a medical emergency usually requiring surgical intervention. They also increase the likelihood that other surgeries will be required during pregnancy, such as cesarean section. The medical interventions of these processes also heighten the chances of infection, miscarriage, sterility, and even death. However, IVF endangers only one woman, not two (if the biological mother provides her own egg).

In the United States the federal government neither registers nor licenses IVF clinics and physicians. This allows a physician to set up a practice specializing in "infertility" treatment even if he or she has had little or no training in reproductive technologies. Other countries, such as Britain and Australia, have regulations regarding IVF and embryo research and require licensure of clinics. For example, in England, in order to acquire a license to perform ICSI, "each clinic must first apply for a research license and perfect the technique on eggs, which must be discarded and not transferred to a woman's uterus. It must do some genuine research in the process, although the results need not be published. Once the clinic can prove the competence of its embryologists, it can apply for a treatment license and begin transferring the injected eggs to the woman." [25]

No such standards exist in the United States or Canada. With little or no training, mistakes are more likely to occur, and patients suffer the consequences. Consider the recent case in New York where a woman was told, while in the operating room awaiting transplantation of the fertilized ovum, that her physician had implanted it previously in another woman. Eventually she sued the physician for malpractice *and lost.* [26] Given the impact reproductive technologies can have on future generations and the experimental nature of the process, standards for licensure, accreditation, and training should be of the utmost stringency. Instead, they are nonexistent.

In Canada, where there are voluntary guidelines but no regulations or licensure requirements, the Royal Commission on New Reproductive Technologies recently conducted an investigation into clinics offering IVF and insemination services.[27] Striking variations were noted, particularly in the amount of record keeping. While some clinics were meticulous, others kept only sketchy records. Poor record keeping makes it difficult to research the effects of IVF on mothers, children, and egg donors. Although parents are not always receptive to follow-up research, it would be easy enough to require them to sign their consent to it at the same time that they sign the consent for treatment. Of course, without regulations it is impossible to standardize any consent or treatment protocols. Currently, some clinics provide very specific consent forms; others, very general ones. Some clinics supply information about risks in language so technical a layperson cannot easily decipher it. The Canadian commission rated the information regarding risks that clinics supplied to patients and found it fair to poor in overall quality.

Although consent forms may not inform couples of the risks and the relative experimental nature of IVF and IVF derivatives, they often limit liability through a variety of clauses. For example, the Virginia clinic that advertised in England, boasting of the availability of egg donors, has couples sign consent forms that state, in part, "If you, or any of your offspring, should require any medical treatment as a result of physical injury arising from embryo cryopreservation and the donor oocyte program, financial responsibility for such care will be yours." [28] In addition, apparently "Before embryos get anywhere near the deep freeze, the customer is required to sign a legal document specifying who will own them if the couple divorces, the woman becomes incapable of bearing a child (through, for example, hysterectomy), or any untoward event occurs." [29] If the couple cannot assume ownership, it falls by default to the clinic.

At Johns Hopkins University, the client must sign a document that sounds like a consent to participation in research:

I understand that my participation may contribute to the general advancement of scientific knowledge that may benefit some individuals in the future. I understand that any information obtained by my use of the fertility drugs may be used in medical studies, however, my name will be kept confidential. I understand that my diagnostic studies will be supervised by one of the investigators and that the Program Director will oversee my care.

I am advised that if physical injury should result from participation in this program, the Johns Hopkins University and Hospital provide no insurance coverage, compensation plan or free medical care plan to compensate me for such injuries.

I understand that photographs of my abdomen, or pelvic organs, may be taken. I understand that the purpose of these photographs is to teach other physicians. I understand that my confidentiality will be protected.[30]

If these procedures are standard, then why do they sound experimental? Moreover, can prospective parents really provide *informed* consent when the possible side effects and ramifications of the procedure remain unknown? Finally, although consent forms can be quite detailed, they rarely address the most common side effects couples experience from IVF: the psychological ones.

The Tumultuous Psychological Experience of IVF

Infertility and infertility treatment has often been described as an emotional "roller-coaster" ride.[31] Imagine a heterosexual couple, with no known fertility problems, beginning their initial attempts at pregnancy. They may begin to note physiological changes in the woman, perhaps take her basal body temperature, check cervical mucus, and even buy an ovulation predictor kit to determine peak fertility. Through the first half of her cycle they eagerly wait for the appropriate time, and through the latter half they eagerly await the results. The first cycle is filled with anticipation and excitement.

This pattern then continues for several months. The process is no longer new or exciting. Looking for signs of ovulation or pregnancy has simply become monotonous, and the couple is becoming desperate. They begin to invest more emotion and perhaps money in the process and anxiously look for more signs of fertility. Intercourse becomes a chore, not a pleasure. The emotional "roller coaster" is just beginning. The "ups" come with each new attempt, the "downs" with the start of each new menstrual cycle. Financial and emotional costs often begin to strain the relationship. They begin to worry if they are victims of the "infertility epidemic." Finally, even if conception does occur, the ride may not be over. The pregnancy may be plagued with complications, or the woman may miscarry. For patients using reproductive technologies, risks are intensified. This is particularly true with IVF and derivatives of IVF, which have increased rates of miscarriage and multiple pregnancies are common.

For an infertile couple, IVF is a gamble. As their investment increases, so does their desperation and desire. It is difficult to give up. Unwittingly, the couple has become enmeshed in the hopes and promises of IVF; they are praying at the altar of science. And they are probably, for the most part, unaware of the extent to which decisions made by others, and for political reasons, will affect their personal and seemingly private reproductive pursuits.

The Politics of IVF

In 1993, Congress and President Clinton approved the National Institutes of Health Revitalization Act of 1993 that affects the cost, effectiveness, and safety of IVF procedures. The bill allows the federal government to fund research on IVF (although in 1994 Clinton ordered that no federal funds were to be used on human embryo research). Why, one wonders, did the government wait so long before funding research on an important procedure that affects the lives of millions?

When the possibility of "test-tube" babies became a reality in the mid-1970s, the Carter administration established a type of institutional review board (IRB) called the Ethics Advisory Board (EAB). The EAB was to review research proposals on IVF and consequently ensure the safety of IVF research participants.[32] Without the approval of the EAB, no research project on IVF could obtain federal funds. Unfortunately, the charter for the EAB lapsed. The subsequent Reagan and Bush administrations never renewed it, thereby effectively stonewalling any federally funded research on IVF and dismantling the board charged with the *ethical* analysis of this and related procedures.

The law President Clinton signed is a mixed blessing. In essence, it eliminates the need for EAB approval before research on IVF can be funded. Therefore, more federally funded research can, and probably will, get under way. However, unless the researcher or institution sponsoring the research has an IRB itself, the welfare of potential research participants will not be the specific focus of anyone's supervision. This could be disastrous. Fortunately, there are plans to create a federal ad hoc advisory panel.[33]

No federal funding was available in the early, critical years of IVF development, so researchers turned to private grantors, such as pharmaceutical companies, that often had a vested interest in the outcome of the research. In the United States alone, infertility treatment is an industry that brings in at least a billion dollars a year. A major portion of the proceeds come from fertility drugs that induce "superovulation" for egg harvesting.

These drugs are also used to synchronize the cycles of the egg donor and the egg recipient and are routine treatment for all types of infertility.

One researcher in Australia, Alan Trounson, has developed a technique that allows physicians to remove immature eggs from the ovary, virtually eliminating the need for extensive use of fertility drugs. After the eggs mature, they are fertilized and implanted in the uterus. At least one child has been born using this method. Economists predict, "If the Trounson procedure becomes routine, it could fundamentally change the IVF business, which derives much of its profit from the prescription of fertility drugs and the monitoring of patients for adverse side-effects. Dr Trounson claims that his technique could save 80–90% of the current costs of IVF in America—up to $10,000 per cycle." [34] Clearly, pharmaceutical companies have a conflict of interest in funding research on prevention or cures for infertility, especially if it involves reducing the use of fertility drugs.

The insurance industry also has a vested interest in IVF procedures. Initially, most health insurers did not provide coverage for IVF,[35] but the states are one by one beginning to mandate it. Insurance companies fought the trend, claiming, among other things, that the procedures are elective and experimental. However, as overall health care costs rose and insurers began losing battles like the one over IVF, they shifted to a new strategy: managed care. Now, where coverage is mandated, insurance companies have begun setting up preferred provider organizations (PPOs), contracting with a selected group of health professionals who agree to provide services for a set (generally reduced) fee. Insurers then offer better coverage for services rendered by their preferred providers than for those rendered by other providers. Clinics and physicians who choose not to become a preferred provider may suffer from a lack of referrals. Providers now compete to offer the lowest cost to insurance contractors. This drives down the expense of IVF and other infertility treatments.

The casualties of such political battles are almost always women. It is women who have suffered the consequences of inadequate or biased research over the last sixteen years. Instead of isolating and identifying the causes of and treatments for infertility, physicians have attempted to develop new technologies to create life. Ironically, these technologies often *cause* female infertility. But couples are lured, by their own hopes and by medical hype, to try, try, and try again.

Frozen Embryos

The mainstream newspaper headlines sound like those of supermarket tabloids: "Timewarp Triplets Born." Guy Hudson, a triplet, was born in July 1994. His sisters had been born three years earlier. In 1991, when the Hudsons underwent IVF, fertilized eggs were implanted in Ms. Hudson's uterus. Guy's sisters were the result. The embryo that would eventually become Guy was cryopreserved and, three years later, was implanted in his mother's uterus. Technically the three siblings are triplets, conceived at the same time but delivered three years apart.[36]

IVF was the first step toward developing the technology necessary for cryopreservation of embryos. Once eggs could be fertilized outside the uterus, it became possible to experiment with freezing fertilized eggs or embryos, thereby preserving them for future implantation. Theoretically, if embryos could be frozen, women might not have to undergo repeated hormone manipulation and egg extraction. Rather, eggs could be removed, fertilized, and stored as embryos, then implanted during subsequent cycles when the woman was undergoing the natural hormonal changes that favor pregnancy.

The first successful pregnancy from a cryopreserved embryo occurred in Australia in 1984. By 1992, there were 19,893 frozen embryos in storage *in Australia alone.*[37] The cryopreservation of embryos is relatively simple. The embryo can be frozen at the pronuclear stage (when it has one cell) or after it has divided two, four, six, or more times.[38] It is dehydrated to prevent the formation of ice crystals that may rupture the membrane and then infused with preservatives, sealed in a tube, and slowly frozen. Approximately 40 to 50 percent of embryos do not survive the freezing process. Those that do are stored in liquid nitrogen, where they can remain for years, perhaps even decades or centuries. As the embryo is thawed for implantation, it is rehydrated.

The pregnancy rate after frozen embryo implantation is about 8 to 12 percent, the actual birth rate only about 6 to 9 percent. Overall, embryos frozen at earlier stages of development have a greater chance of thriving after implantation. Twins and triplets have often been born from frozen embryos. Additionally, other IVF techniques have been successfully combined with cryopreservation. For example, a successful birth resulted from a frozen embryo created with a donor egg. Another child was born from a frozen embryo that had originally been fertilized through the ICSI technique (the injection of a single sperm into the egg). Embryo cryopreservation has also created remarkable, often bizarre scenarios that generate complex legal, moral, and medical dilemmas.

The Legal Status of Frozen Embryos

Even before the first successful birth from a frozen embryo, the courts were debating the legal status of frozen embryos in a very

unusual and highly publicized case. Elsa and Mario Rios wanted
to have a child. Mario had a son from a previous marriage, but
Elsa was childless. In 1981, the Rioses traveled from California
to Australia to undergo IVF. The procedure was not successful,
but two of their embryos were frozen. In 1983, both Mario and
Elsa were killed in a plane crash, leaving a multimillion-dollar
estate and two frozen embryos. Mario's son stood to inherit the
estate, but his claim would have been jeopardized if any children
were produced from the frozen embryos. The court sought to
determine the inheritance rights of the embryos, but when it was
learned that Mario's vasectomy had rendered him infertile and
the semen that fertilized the eggs had come from an anonymous
donor, the inheritance issue was rendered moot. The embryos
were reportedly donated to an infertile couple.

When a case involving a frozen embryo comes to the attention of the legal system, it usually revolves around "ownership"
of the embryo. This becomes a very complicated issue. Initially
the courts must decide if the embryo is a human life or not.[39] If
the courts decide that the embryo is a human "life," they next
must decide whether it has rights that must be protected. If it
does, the courts may decide to exercise their parens patriae
power, that is, to make decisions in the "best interests of the
child." However, if the embryo is not a human "life," then
"ownership" of it should be guided by the laws of property. The
debate was illustrated in the case of *Davis v. Davis*.[40]

Mary Sue and Junior Davis attempted to have a baby "naturally" for several years. After several ectopic pregnancies, Mary
Sue was advised to have her fallopian tubes removed, thus
preventing "natural" conception. The Davises then underwent
several unsuccessful IVF treatments. In December 1988, two of
the Davises' embryos were unsuccessfully implanted in Mary
Sue Davis, and the remaining seven were cryopreserved. In Feb-

ruary 1989, the Davises separated, and Junior sued for divorce. The only disputed items in the marital dissolution were the frozen embryos.

Mary Sue wanted to implant the embryos in herself or donate them to another infertile couple (she later changed her mind regarding donation). Junior wanted the embryos to remain frozen or be destroyed. He maintained that he did not want any children of his to issue from a "broken" home, as his own upbringing in an institutional home for boys had been unpleasant. Furthermore, Junior argued, to allow any of the embryos to become a full-fledged child would be to force him into parenthood against his will and make him financially responsible for a child he did not want. In other words, he argued that he had a fundamental right *not* to procreate.

Apparently, Junior was attempting to use a variation of the arguments presented before the United States Supreme Court in *Roe v. Wade* (1973). In *Roe v. Wade,* the Supreme Court held that women had the right to abort a fetus in the first trimester of pregnancy. In that case, the Court had to determine if the interests of the state in a prospective, potentially productive member of society (the fetus) were compelling enough to override the fundamental right of the pregnant woman, derived from the Fourteenth Amendment, which has been interpreted as providing a right to privacy. In *Roe v. Wade,* the Supreme Court ruled that the right to privacy included the right to bodily autonomy and that forcing a woman to carry a fetus against her will infringed on her right to bodily autonomy and therefore her right to privacy. They did not determine that women had a fundamental right *not to* procreate. Rather, in the case of abortion, the woman's right to privacy and bodily autonomy *superseded* the rights of the fetus and the state's interest in the fetus.

In order to concede Junior's argument, that he had a fundamental right *not to* procreate, implantation of the embryos would have to infringe on his bodily autonomy, his right to privacy. But the embryos existed outside of Junior Davis's body. Unless he could argue that the embryos were extensions of his body—a dubious contention—Junior would not necessarily have a right to destroy them. If he couldn't argue this, his right to destroy them depended on whether the embryos were considered "persons" or property. If the embryos were deemed to be a form of human life, the court could apply its parens patriae standard to protect them, and the case would be resolved under family law principles. If the embryos represent property, the case should be resolved under the principles of property law. Mary Sue argued that if the embryos did represent property, she had a greater interest in the "property" because she had a greater investment in their creation. After all, she underwent hormone manipulation, surgery, and egg aspiration (harvesting), while Junior simply supplied the semen.

Initially, the court ruled in favor of Mary Sue, declaring that life begins at conception. Therefore, the court could use the parens patriae standard to "protect" the embryos. The appeals court overturned this decision, using a more property-based analysis. The Tennessee Supreme Court upheld the appeals court decision in favor of Junior. However, the Tennessee Supreme Court did not use a property analysis. The Tennessee Supreme Court held that disputes should be settled according to the preferences of the gamete providers. If the preferences are in dispute, the court indicated, prior existing agreements should be upheld. If, as in the Davis case, no prior agreement exists, then the court ruled that the "relative interests" of the parties should be balanced. The Tennessee Supreme Court indicated that their decision might have been different if it had determined that the party objecting to destruction (Mary Sue) had no other "reasonable alternatives" for conception and pregnancy in the future (i.e., that she was infertile). Then destruction of the embryos would interfere with her fundamental right to procreate. The United States Supreme Court refused to hear the case. Junior then destroyed the embryos.

If the embryo represents a human life, this could become an insurmountable obstacle to medical research on, or even performance of, the IVF procedure. Theoretically, physicians could no longer conduct research using embryos or discard fresh or frozen embryos, because to do so could be considered murder. In fact, with an 85 to 90 percent failure rate, IVF itself may be considered involuntary manslaughter.

Interestingly, antichoice forces have been relatively silent on the frozen-embryo issue. Even though the Davis case turned on the issue of when life begins—the central issue for antichoice groups—the plight of frozen embryos has not and probably never will create controversy proportionate to the abortion debate. It's unlikely that infertility clinics will be picketed or infertility doctors murdered because embryos are destroyed at the facility. Perhaps this is due to general ignorance about the process. Or perhaps a gender distinction is at work: abortion relates to women's fundamental right to procreate or not to procreate, whereas destruction of embryos, since it is generally requested by men, involves *men's* fundamental right to procreate or not to procreate.

Generally, when "ownership" of embryos is contested, the dispute occurs between the biological parents. Usually the biological "mother" wants to implant or donate the embryos and the biological "father" wants to destroy them (for fear of being asked to take responsibility for the children that could result from them). However, in *York v. Jones,* the clinic fought both biological parents for custody of the embryos.

Steven and Riza York underwent IVF at the Howard and Georgeanna Jones Institute for Reproductive Medicine in Virginia from 1986 to 1987. In 1987, six eggs were removed from

Riza York and fertilized by Steven's semen. Five were implanted in Riza's uterus; one was cryopreserved. None of the initial implantations was successful. When the Yorks moved to California, they wanted to transfer the one remaining frozen embryo to a clinic in California. The Virginia clinic refused, arguing that the Yorks had signed a consent stipulating that the embryo be implanted at the Virginia clinic. The clinic indicated that the Yorks could donate the embryo for research or to another couple or have it destroyed but could not transport it. They voiced a number of concerns over releasing embryos to clients, including the possibility that an embryo could be damaged, lost, or stolen. The Yorks maintained that the clinic was holding the embryo "hostage." On the eve of trial, the clinic agreed to release the embryo to the Yorks and to compensate them, to some extent, for their legal expenses. The Yorks agreed not to hold the clinic liable for anything that might happen to the embryo and to take full responsibility for it. Steven York bought a seat on a flight to California for the liquid nitrogen tank containing the embryo and transported it to the California clinic. Later attempts to implant the embryo proved unsuccessful.

Many clinics are beginning to require biological parents to make provisions for any frozen embryos prior to undergoing IVF. However, several problems remain. First, the legality of such provisions has never been contested, so it is still uncertain how binding they really are. When custody provisions made in a will (for existing children) have been challenged, they have been disregarded by the court. Custody contracts between sperm donors and sperm recipients and between "surrogate" mothers and contracting parties have also been invalidated or disregarded. Second, such contracts cannot fully encompass all the possible scenarios that can unfold around a frozen embryo. Finally, couples can always maintain that circumstances have changed so drastically that the contract they signed has been invalidated.[41]

Controversial, precedent-setting cases continue to be filed. In 1994, a Long Island couple were in the process of a divorce and disputed "ownership" of frozen embryos created in May 1993. Maureen Kass, a Catholic, argued that the destruction of the embryos would violate her religious beliefs and, moreover, that she had no other "reasonable alternatives" for procreation, because she is sterile. This had been an important factor in *Davis v. Davis,* where the court ruled that frozen embryos might be used over the objections of a potential parent if no "reasonable alternatives" for pregnancy remained for the parent attempting to retain the embryos. In their divorce agreement, the Kasses agreed, regarding the embryos, to abide by the decision of a justice of the Supreme Court of New York. In contrast to the ruling in *Davis,* a Nassau County judge ruled in favor of Maureen Kass in January 1995. Maureen said that she would have the embryos implanted within a month. Steven, her ex-husband, said he would appeal.

The Medical and Ethical Status of Frozen Embryos

Medical and ethical issues become particularly intertwined when one is dealing with frozen embryos. The medical procedures and technology involved in freezing embryos create new ethical dilemmas. For example, if IVF or subsequent implantation with a frozen embryo is successful, numerous other embryos, harvested at the same time, may remain in liquid nitrogen indefinitely. Some prospective parents want to keep these embryos in frozen storage as insurance, in case something happens to their child(ren).[42] Some clinics assess couples monthly or yearly "storage" fees. It is unclear what happens when couples want to retain their embryos but cannot afford the storage costs.

Since embryos can remain frozen indefinitely, it is theoretically possible for biological parents to have a child (gestated by someone else) decades after they are deceased. Since the technology that makes it possible to produce live births from cryopreserved embryos is barely a decade old, a situation of this sort has not yet actually occurred, but it could. The AFS can only *recommend,* not mandate, that embryos be stored for no more than five years (certainly not beyond the reproductive life span of the couple).

A related issue is the status of embryos after prospective parents decide to cancel their "insurance policy." The embryos could be donated to another infertile couple, destroyed, or used for experimentation. If they are donated to another infertile couple, the "adoptive" couple will obviously have no genetic link to the embryos, and it could be argued that they might as well have adopted an infant or child already born. The only additional benefit to "adopting" an embryo and attempting IVF would be the gestational link between the "adoptive" parents and the embryo. This hardly seems worth the cost. Also, since the parents of donated embryos, like egg and sperm donors, are not registered on any central list, the possibility of a marriage between siblings can never be precluded. One could limit the number of a given couple's embryos that can be frozen or prohibit the further use of a couple's embryos after a set number of successful births. However, the problem of surplus would remain.

For parents who have gone to extreme measures, such as trying IVF in order to have children, it must be difficult indeed to decide whether to have their frozen embryos destroyed. In some states and countries the couple would not be given this choice: legislation protects the embryo from destruction. Similarly, some states and countries legislate against the use of nontherapeutic procedures (i.e., experimentation) on fetuses or embryos. But such legislative protection is relatively rare, and within the next few years, as IVF and cryopreservation become more popular and storage space increasingly scarce, many individuals may be forced to decide the fate of their could-be children.

A Last Look at Regulations

During late May 1995, a scandal began to unfold at the University of California at Irvine's Center for Reproductive Health. On 2 June, the university accused three of the center's physicians, each a world-renowned fertility expert (one was the physician who perfected GIFT), of breach of ethics and contract. The physicians were accused of prescribing an unapproved fertility drug and performing research on clients without their consent. The university also alleged that in approximately thirty cases, the physicians removed frozen embryos from storage without the biological parents' consent and implanted them in other patients. It is estimated that up to seven children were born from these implantations. These children may never know their biological parents and the biological parents may never know their children. The physicians maintain that it was other staff who bungled the embryo transfers. Though they violated professional guidelines, these physicians have not violated any regulations or California laws. In a separate incident, two lawsuits were filed against a Rhode Island clinic in July and August of 1995. That clinic is accused of "losing" nine embryos, six belonging to one couple and three to another couple. Of course, these embryos could also have been "mistakenly" given to the wrong patients, although the clinic denies that this happened.

A few states have laws regarding the disposition of embryos or experimentation with them or even regarding the required record keeping. However, these laws are sparse and far from comprehensive.[43] Very little movement has been made toward licensure or the regulation of standards. Few politicians want to become entangled in an issue that contains components of the abortion controversy and might thus arouse vehement responses from many Americans. Furthermore, any proposal to regulate the medical profession invariably ignites the wrath of the American Medical Association, a powerful lobby and a generous campaign contributor.

Proposals to regulate IVF and related technologies raise another issue, highlighted by the Davis case. Does regulation of reproductive technologies infringe on a person's fundamental rights? The governments of Australia and England apparently do not think so, or do not feel that the infringement is so serious that it should take precedence over other considerations. However, the political climate of each of these countries is very different from that of the United States.

Let us assume for a moment that regulating reproductive technologies *does* interfere with fundamental rights. Does not, however, a lack of regulation also interfere with an individual's fundamental rights? For the infertile, these rights remain illusory in the absence of regulation, since high costs and/or discriminatory methods of selecting "appropriate" clients rule out a great many potential parents. Furthermore, major decisions, such as which fetuses will be selectively aborted, are left to physicians. In the United States, the medical profession enjoys relatively free rein regarding reproductive technologies. Regulation would bring a wider and more representative group of individuals into the picture, who, with their more varied interests and areas of expertise, might be better able to assess without bias the best interests of all parties. It is ironic that the country that is perhaps the largest provider of IVF services should lag the furthest behind in research and regulation.

"Wombs for Rent"

When infertility stems from a malfunction of the woman's reproductive system, the woman or couple sometimes resort to surrogacy.[44] "Partial surrogacy" has been practiced for centuries. When a woman could not bear a child, another woman agreed (or was forced) to become impregnated with the sperm of the woman's partner and carry the child to term. In fact, in the Bible, handmaids gave birth for Sarah, Rachel, and Leah when they could not conceive.[45] In this case, the "surrogate" is termed a partial surrogate: because she supplies the egg, so she is "partially" the "mother."

With the advent of in vitro fertilization, "full surrogacy," in which the "surrogate" simply gestates the fetus but has no genetic connection to it, became possible. The gametes of a woman and a man are combined in vitro, and any resulting embryos are then implanted in the uterus of a third person, the "surrogate." Women who have ovaries and ova but are rendered infertile by hysterectomy or uterine malfunction can now have a biological child, although they do not actually undergo the pregnancy. In a variation of this process, termed surrogate embryo transfer, the embryo is conceived by the genetic mother, then "flushed" from her uterus and implanted within a full "surrogate's" uterus. This procedure can be used when a biological mother is able to conceive but not to gestate a fetus. Finally, in embryo transfer, the embryo is conceived within the "surrogate" (using her egg), then "flushed" from the "surrogate's" body and implanted in the uterus of a gestational mother. Therefore, the "surrogate's" role is similar to an egg donor. For the remainder of the chapter, the term "surrogacy" will be used to refer both to full and partial surrogacy.

In surrogacy situations, any resulting children are supposed to be surrendered to the contracting parents after the birth.

Generally, "surrogates" receive between ten and fifteen thousand dollars as payment for their "services," which may include extensive screening, inseminations, pregnancy, and childbirth. The contracting couple may pay as much as fifty thousand dollars when agency, medical, insurance, and surrogacy costs are totaled, two to three times the cost of a typical adoption.

While all reproductive technologies have created some controversy, surrogacy has ignited a virtual firestorm. More laws, lawsuits, and law review articles have been touched off by surrogacy than by any other reproductive technology. Additionally, there are more books on surrogacy than on insemination, IVF, and frozen embryos combined. Debates continue over numerous issues, including whether surrogates should be paid, whether the whole concept amounts to slavery, whether children are being sold, whether the process itself should be prohibited, and whether prohibiting it violates constitutional rights. Surrogacy arouses the wrath of some feminists, the curiosity of the general public, and the concern of legal scholars, ethicists, and religious groups.

The Legal System and Surrogacy

It is estimated that over five thousand children have been born through surrogacy contracting in the United States alone. The most celebrated and misunderstood case involving surrogacy was the case of Baby M (see below). However, Baby M was not the first child born of a surrogate mother. "Attorney Noel Keane, the self-proclaimed 'father of surrogate motherhood,' first got the idea when Jane and her husband Tom visited him in September 1976. Tom had 'this harebrained idea of finding another woman to carry a child for them' (Jane was infertile) but didn't know how to go about it." [46]

Nor was Baby M the first surrogacy case to come to the attention of the legal system.[47] In 1980, Denise Thrane was inseminated with sperm from James Noyes, whose wife could not become pregnant.[48] Eventually Thrane changed her mind about surrendering the baby and the Noyeses sued for custody. The Noyeses relented when they learned that Thrane had discovered that Mrs. Noyes was a transsexual, a factor that they believed might jeopardize their bid for custody.

In 1982, when a "surrogate" gave birth to a child with microcephaly, which resulted in mental retardation, hearing loss, and neuromuscular disorders, all parents/prospective parents renounced custody.[49] The microcephaly resulted from cytomegalovirus (CMV), a sexually transmitted disease. Although it was determined that the surrogate's husband was actually the genetic father of the child, the surrogate maintained that the contracting husband provided the semen that caused the CMV infection. The surrogate and her husband later sued the physicians and attorneys involved in the case (including Noel Keane) for not testing the semen used in inseminations for sexually transmitted diseases, thereby not fulfilling their duty to protect.

Most surrogacy contracting arrangements are completed with little fanfare and often with positive results. However, when there is controversy, it is always well publicized. In 1984, Mary Beth Whitehead applied to Noel Keane's Infertility Center to become a "surrogate mother." Her motivation was partially altruistic. She intended to use the ten-thousand-dollar fee to finance her children's college education. As a part of the application process, Whitehead was "screened" by a psychiatrist, who came to the conclusion that Whitehead might have difficulty relinquishing a child and recommended further counseling. The center chose to disregard this information and proceeded with inseminations. Eventually, Whitehead was impregnated with sperm from William Stern. Neither Whitehead nor the Sterns were informed of the cautions from the "screening."

William and Elizabeth Stern had postponed having children. They both had doctoral degrees, and Elizabeth had a medical degree as well. When Elizabeth learned that she had a mild case of multiple sclerosis and that pregnancy would exacerbate the condition, the Sterns sought the services of a surrogate. Facilities providing full surrogacy were difficult to find, so the Sterns agreed to partial surrogacy. The Sterns met the Whiteheads, and the contract was drawn up. The Whiteheads agreed to name William as the father on the birth certificate, not to abort the baby unless the amniocentesis revealed abnormalities, and to surrender custody to the Sterns. The Sterns agreed to pay the Whiteheads ten thousand dollars for a live birth, one thousand dollars if Ms. Whitehead miscarried after the fourth month.

In the early stages of pregnancy, the Sterns and the Whiteheads became quite close but the relationship became strained when the Sterns insisted that Mary Beth undergo amniocentesis and get more bed rest. On 27 March 1986, Whitehead gave birth to Melissa Stern/Sara Whitehead. She did not name William Stern as the father on the birth certificate but rather her own husband. Nor did she immediately surrender the child. Whitehead allegedly called Noel Keane and indicated that she could not follow through on the agreement.[50] He reportedly told her to take her baby home, that at most the Sterns would seek visitation rights. However, William Stern, who had lost most of his family in the Holocaust, was not about to give up his child without a fight. Three days later Whitehead surrendered the baby to the Sterns. The next day she returned and pleaded to keep the baby for a week longer. The Sterns reluctantly agreed.

What followed was perfect fodder for a made-for-TV movie.

The Whiteheads left with the child, hid out in hotels, and were eventually arrested and brought back to New Jersey. The Sterns were granted temporary custody of the child, but Mary Beth Whitehead was allowed to visit her. At the trial court, the judge held that the contract between the Sterns and the Whiteheads was enforceable and awarded custody to the Sterns. The New Jersey appeals court found the contract unenforceable, because it amounted to "baby selling," which violated adoption statutes and public policy. However, custody was awarded to the Sterns anyway, and Mary Beth Whitehead retained visitation rights.

In California in 1993, a case addressing the rights of a "full (or gestational) surrogate" was decided. Crispina Calvert was unable to gestate a fetus, since she had undergone a hysterectomy in 1984. However, Crispina still had her ovaries. She and her husband, Mark, decided to find a surrogate to gestate an embryo produced from Crispina's egg and Mark's sperm. Anna Johnson agreed to serve as a surrogate for the couple, and on 15 January 1990, all parties signed a contract wherein Anna agreed to relinquish her rights to the child in return for $10,000. The Calverts were also to supply a $200,000 life insurance policy for Ms. Johnson. Eventually, the relationship between the parties began to deteriorate. The Calverts learned that Johnson had deceived them regarding her obstetric history. Johnson felt that the Calverts had abandoned her during a bout of premature labor and that they had not put enough effort into securing insurance. When Johnson intimated that she would not give up the child, the Calverts countered with a lawsuit to establish their parental rights.[51]

After the child was born, temporary custody was awarded to the Calverts (after genetic tests determined that they were the biological parents). Ms. Johnson was temporarily awarded visitation rights. The trial court found that the contract was enforceable, determined that the Calverts were the child's "genetic, biological and natural parents," and terminated Ms. Johnson's visitation rights. The verdict was upheld by the appeals and supreme courts of California. The United States Supreme Court refused to hear the case. The Calverts later sued Johnson and the surrogacy firm for fraud, breach of contract, and infliction of emotional distress. Although they dropped the suit against Johnson, they received an undisclosed amount from the surrogacy firm.[52]

Just as the courts grapple with which law applies to frozen embryos, family law or property law, so must they grapple with which law applies to surrogacy contracts, family law or contract law. If surrogacy contracts represent family law, then the best-interests-of-the-child standard applies. However, by the standards of contract law, the first question is enforceability.

If the contract amounts to "baby selling," then it is unenforceable, because it conflicts with a number of adoption statutes and with public policy. It is a crime in *all* states to surrender a child for a fee. Some states interpret surrogacy contracts as baby selling, and therefore unenforceable, unless no fee is involved. Other states view surrogacy contracts simply as service contracts. In an effort to resolve these conflicts, over half of the states have proposed surrogacy legislation since 1980.[53] However, the laws that have been enacted vary tremendously.

Some states ban surrogacy contracting altogether, while others ban commercial surrogacy contracts—those involving payment—with civil and/or criminal penalties for violators. Other states ban compensation for the surrogate agency or surrogacy broker, providing criminal penalties for violations. Still others have attempted to regulate custody or parentage, that is, whether the gestational or the biological mother is the legal mother. At least one state has a statutory provision that allows surrogates to change their mind about surrendering the baby for up to seventy-two hours postpartum. Some countries also have regulations regarding surrogacy.

These statutes raise questions regarding sexism and gender equity. Many state statutes address and/or limit compensation to women for surrogacy. Supposedly, these laws are designed to prevent the commodification of babies and women's reproductive capacities. However, this concern only seems to arise when females, not males, are compensated for marketing their reproductive capacities. Females are expected to become surrogates for strictly altruistic motives. Rarely does anyone question whether sperm donors should be *repeatedly* compensated for their "product," yet egg donors and surrogates are scrutinized. Clearly the "product" and the process are different for sperm donors and surrogates, but the concept is similar. "Women's work," it seems, is not worth compensating. The irony is that the compensation to the surrogate is so limited that the agency/broker generally ends up making the windfall profit. However, most states are not clamoring to limit agency/broker profits.

State statutes also tend to propose simplistic solutions to complex problems. For example, in Arizona, Pamela and Ronald Soos contracted for a full surrogacy. Pamela had previously had a partial hysterectomy that left her with ovaries but no uterus. Pamela and Ronald underwent IVF, and the embryos that resulted were implanted in a surrogate. Unfortunately, the Sooses divorced before the birth of the children (triplets), and when they were born, the surrogate gave temporary custody to Ronald. Under an Arizona surrogacy law, the surrogate is the legal mother of the child. Similarly, other states have laws declaring that oocyte donors (which is what Pamela was, in essence) have no rights to custody. Since her ex-husband had temporary custody and she had no legal rights, Pamela was unable to see her genetic offspring for three months. Apparently the Arizona statute presumes that the husband of the surrogate is the father of the child unless this presumption is challenged by a paternity test from the genetic father. No comparable provision permits genetic mothers to challenge maternity. Pamela Soos challenged this statute, and it was struck down by the appeals court as unconstitutional. Pamela can now continue her fight for custody, while Ronald vows to appeal the ruling.

Conversely, in *Johnson v. Calvert* the court held that the genetic mother was the legal mother. Again, this represents a simplistic solution to a complex problem, setting a potentially disastrous precedent for future decisions. If the genetic mother is the legal mother, then egg donors would have a legal claim to children produced from their donations unless they relinquished their parental rights *after* the birth of the child.

As with all statutes that vary from state to state, such as those that concern gambling or abortion, surrogacy regulations simply invite individuals desiring specific surrogacy options to travel to a state that permits them. Strict regulation can also drive the process underground, which does not serve anyone's interest. On the other hand, states without any legislation in this area only add to the confusion, forcing each judge to apply his or her own personal principles to resolve the cases that come before the courts.

On a theoretical level, the regulation of surrogacy contracts raises constitutional issues as well. For example, regulation of surrogacy contracting could interfere with an individual's right to contract. Legal scholars debate whether the fundamental right to procreate, derived from the right to privacy, includes a fundamental right to privacy in surrogacy contracting. If so, the state could not regulate surrogacy contracts without demonstrating an interest compelling enough to override an individual's fundamental rights. In short, the question of regulating surrogacy is enormously complex. Existing regulations have not been challenged on constitutional grounds, and a constitutional challenge could prove quite successful. Overall, it is apparent that, for surrogacy legislation to be effective, it must be more consistent, less invasive, and federal.

Ethical Concerns

A person's attitude toward surrogacy often depends on what aspect of it has engaged his or her attention. For example, some individuals express support for surrogacy because they believe that everyone has a constitutional right to procreation or to surrogacy contracting. Conversely, some individuals oppose surrogacy for ethical reasons. As with all the reproductive technologies, the ethical and moral dilemmas surrounding surrogacy are limitless.

Numerous organizations have adopted guidelines regarding surrogacy.[54] The American College of Obstetricians and Gynecologists (ACOG) indicated that it had "significant reservations" regarding the procedure and offered recommendations for physicians. The American Medical Association (AMA) does not "endorse [or] condemn surrogate parenting" but advises practitioners to use "great care and discretion." The American Fertility Society (AFS) advised "intense scrutiny" of all surrogacy situations. They cautioned against the use of surrogacy for nonmedical reasons and discouraged widespread use of surrogacy by medical practitioners. Furthermore, the committee suggested that if surrogacy were undertaken, "it should be pursued as a clinical experiment." Finally, the AFS advised physicians to obtain fully informed consents and to avoid a conflict of interests by not accepting payments beyond their customary fees.

The American Civil Liberties Union (ACLU) also elaborates their position on surrogacy in a detailed document. The ACLU holds that the state does not have a right to ban surrogacy agreements and that compensation for surrogacy is acceptable as long as payment is not contingent on the surrogate relinquishing her rights. The ACLU also offers guidelines for the determination of custody and parental rights in surrogacy cases.

Unfortunately, guidelines have not provided ironclad answers to ethical problems. What if, for example, the circumstances of the contracting couple radically change, as in the case of a divorce? The Moschettas entered into a surrogacy contract with Elvira Jordan. In 1990, when Jordan was six months pregnant, the Moschettas began discussing divorce but did not inform Jordan until the day before she gave birth. Jordan refused to give up the child, Marissa, unless the couple agreed to marriage counseling. The couple received counseling and cared for Marissa for six months. Then Robert Moschetta took the baby and left his wife. The only definitive ruling that has come from the California court is that Cynthia Moschetta cannot be Marissa's mother because she has no biological relationship to Marissa.[55] The custody decisions and inheritance rights of a child born after contracting parents have died are similarly unclear.

It is also difficult to determine who, in surrogacy situations, is responsible for unwanted children. What if a physically or mentally challenged child or an unexpected twin or triplet results from a surrogacy arrangement and is unwanted by all parties? Most surrogacy contracts have clauses that attempt to assign responsibility for "less-than-perfect" children. Often these clauses limit the contracting parents' responsibility. In 1986, a woman agreed to act as a surrogate for her sister. The surrogate neglected to inform her sister of her history of intravenous drug use. When the child was born HIV-positive, all parties refused responsibility for the child, and the child was placed in social service agencies.

Who is responsible for a child born with a physical or mental defect due to faulty prenatal care—the surrogate or the contracting parents? If the contracting parents attempt to dictate the prenatal regimen of a surrogate (for example, by forbidding alcohol consumption or smoking), does the surrogacy contract amount to indentured servitude?

Finally, if a surrogate's health is seriously jeopardized by the pregnancy, who, if anyone, is liable? In 1987, Denise Mounce was in her eighth month of a surrogate pregnancy when she died of a heart attack at the age of twenty-four. Apparently, Denise required a heart monitor, which her physicians told her she would have to purchase for herself. She could not afford it, and, allegedly, her physicians did not want to "cut into their profits" by purchasing it for her.[56] The physicians and the agency were sued for medical malpractice.

Exploitation vs. Autonomy

Feminists are divided over the issue of surrogacy. On the one hand, surrogacy is viewed as simply another way to exploit and degrade women, potentially turning those of low socioeconomic status into a class of "breeders."

> The core reality of surrogate motherhood is that it is both classist and sexist: a method to obtain children genetically related to white males by exploiting poor women. While it is promoted as simply supplying babies for those who "desperately" want them, in fact it subverts any principled notion of economic fairness and justice, and undermines our commitment to equality and the inherently priceless value of human life.[57]

Conversely, some feminists argue that women should have the right to enter into contracts and that those contracts should be enforced. By not enforcing surrogacy contracts, women's overall capacity to contract could be diminished. After all, if a contract a woman enters into regarding her own body cannot be enforced, why should any contract she enters into be enforced?

Proponents of surrogacy contracting also argue that it is demeaning to women for the government to design legislation that "protects" them from their own choices. In addition, many feminists fear that regulating surrogacy may undermine the right to bodily autonomy that women fought so hard to acquire. Ultimately, "the rationales that they [the feminists who favor regulation] and others are using to justify this governmental intrusion into reproductive choice may come back to haunt feminists in other areas of procreative policy and family law." [58]

The Future of Surrogacy

The interest in surrogacy seems to be waning as we approach the end of the century. Interest peaked in 1988 with the Baby M case and has diminished since, due to a number of factors. As reproductive technologies have advanced, fewer couples need to resort to surrogacy in order to have a child. Restrictive legislation may also have curtailed interest. It is also possible that the publicity surrounding Baby M has discouraged prospective couples from attempting surrogacy, or they may be asking family members to act as surrogates rather than contract with strangers. Perhaps society is simply more accepting of surrogacy now, so it receives less attention from the media.

As public interest has faded, the concern of legislators has likewise diminished. This is unfortunate, since alternatives to simply banning surrogacy or banning commercial surrogacy have rarely been explored. For example, states could regulate the screening/counseling of surrogates and contracting parents, and the results of these preliminary investigations could be considered by all parties when determining whether to proceed. Screening is not always effective and may not eliminate disastrous outcomes, but it does make them less likely. If the results of the screening procedures had been available to all parties in the Baby M case, the entire fiasco might have been avoided. Many issues could be addressed in the screening of prospective parents, such as parenting motivations and the stability of the relationship. Couples who wish to adopt discuss these issues and more during their home study process. In fact, Elizabeth Bartholet, a professor of law at Harvard, believes that parties involved in surrogacy contracts should be regulated more and adoptive parents less.[59] She maintains that the lax regulation of IVF and its derivatives lures people into choosing these procedures rather than adoption, since adoption criteria are so rigorous. In addition, some states have health care coverage for IVF while providing no financial incentives for adoption, not even tax breaks. Finally, physicians often advocate medical solutions to infertility instead of encouraging nonmedical alternatives like adoption. They seem to view infertility as a medical challenge and give little thought to the social ramifications of their recommendations.

Other proposals for regulation have been advanced over the years. Martha Field suggests that regulations address the amount of confidentiality between the parties, requiring either open or closed agreements[60] and that minimum ages for surrogates be set. However, legislators seem to approach surrogacy with an all-or-nothing attitude that forces legal systems (i.e., the courts) and individuals into making difficult choices.

Misplaced Focus

In the midst of all the concern for individual rights and regulations, the best interests of the child seem to have faded from the agenda. Relatively little research has been conducted into the effects of reproductive technologies on children, either physically or psychologically. On the part of both physicians and parents, this represents the ultimate in narcissistic behavior.

Technological efforts to solve the infertility "problem" have intensified. The development of new, more powerful, more invasive means to create life has generated more interest than alleviating or eliminating the causes of infertility. For example, researchers have begun to experiment with increasing the success of IVF through cloning. Once an embryo divides into two cells, the cells can be separated and allowed to develop into twins. Other research is being conducted on ovarian grafting. In ovarian grafting, the cortex of the ovary, which contains the eggs, is removed, frozen, and later replaced. These are complicated and risky procedures that push the limits of nature and endanger women and potential children. Wouldn't it be simpler, safer, and of broader benefit to humankind, to target potential sources of infertility, such as chlamydia?

Chlamydia, a sexually transmitted disease, exists in epidemic proportions; it is insidious and frequently goes undetected. Often the infection results in scarring of the fallopian tubes, which prevents eggs from passing into the uterus and thus causes infertility. Perhaps more emphasis should be placed on alleviating chlamydia through prevention and education than on finding medical ways to bypass its results. Not only would this attenuate infertility but it would also greatly diminish a public health hazard that affects men, women, and children.

Perhaps more research emphasis should be placed on perfecting existing medical interventions, and avoiding the unwanted consequences of some of them, than on developing new technologies. It should not be overlooked that infertility is sometimes iatrogenic, the result of medical intervention. Of course science must progress, but not without regard for the consequences, to the individual and to society, of its experiments.

[3]

Politics and the Control of Women's Bodies

ᖇᖇ

*A*mericans are becoming more health-conscious. Smoking is now prohibited or restricted in most public facilities. Membership in a health club is de rigueur for the monied classes. Shoppers have begun to read the labels on food products, and the FDA has begun to require manufacturers to provide more in-depth nutritional information on those labels. No- or low-fat and no- or low-cholesterol foods are in vogue. Extensive educational and motivational campaigns endorsing "wellness" have been launched all over the country. Some universities even require students to complete courses on "wellness" as part of their general education. Many behaviors that were pitched as healthy twenty years ago, such as eating red meat, are no longer considered "heart smart."

This focus on health and wellness has come to include the fetus. Many substances once considered relatively harmless are now known to affect the developing fetus. All containers of

alcoholic beverages now carry a label starkly reminding pregnant women that the use of alcohol during pregnancy can cause
birth defects. Babies born with birth defects from maternal alcohol use may have been classified simply as mentally retarded in
the past, but fetal alcohol syndrome is now a distinct diagnosis.
In fact, alcohol use during pregnancy is one of the leading causes
of birth defects in the United States.

The response of pregnant women to these newfound teratogens (substances, processes, or agents that can cause defects or
malfunctions in a developing fetus) has paralleled the overall
response of the public to health warnings: some have chosen to
modify their behavior, while others have made no lifestyle
changes. However, the societal and legislative responses when
pregnant women ignore warnings about possible teratogens differ drastically from the corresponding responses to other individual's choice of a potentially unhealthy lifestyle. Consider the
following example:

> Danita Fitch, 21, and G. R. Heryford, 22, were fired from a
> suburban Red Robin restaurant when they tried to stop a patron
> Heryford described as "very pregnant" from having a drink
> March 13.
>
> Jim Roths, Red Robin's director of operations, said Heryford
> and Fitch were fired because they did not treat the customer with
> "respect and dignity."
>
> Heryford said Tuesday he first tried to stop the woman from
> drinking by demanding identification. "I was hoping she didn't
> have it," he said. "Then I could legally refuse her service."
>
> He went to assistant manager Mike Buckley after finding out
> the woman was 30. Buckley ordered him to serve the drink.
> Instead, Heryford told Fitch about the situation and she ap-
> proached the woman.
>
> "I went up to her and said, 'Ma'am, are you sure you want
> this drink?'" Fitch said. "And she got really mad and said, 'It's
> past due. It had its chance.'"

Then, Fitch peeled from a beer bottle the government warning against alcohol consumption by pregnant women and showed it to the patron, who complained to Buckley. The two were then fired.

Heryford said Buckley told them their job was not to lecture customers or offer opinions on prenatal care.

Fitch and Heryford say they hope the state Liquor Control Board will set a policy on serving alcohol to pregnant women.[1]

Some people believe that when a woman becomes pregnant she loses the right to make her own lifestyle choices. These beliefs echo the main controversy regarding many reproductive rights of women, particularly abortion. The question of who has control over a pregnant woman's body remains the subject of extensive debate. The use of substances by pregnant women reflects this controversy. On the one hand, if a woman has reproductive autonomy, this decision can and should be hers alone. On the other hand, for some the use of substances during pregnancy is contingent on the effect the substance may have on the developing fetus and/or eventual child.

Typical Substances Used during Pregnancy

Each year in the United States, an estimated 11 percent of babies are born after exposure to illegal and legal drugs in utero. (This is probably an underestimate, since not all women are tested for substance abuse and many deny it even when drug tests come back positive.) Most substances that are abused fall into one of four categories: depressants, stimulants, narcotics (opioid/morphine derivatives), and hallucinogens. Excluding hallucinogens, which are largely illegal, recreational drugs, the other categories include legal and illegal drugs, some of which can be obtained with a prescription or even over the counter. Of course, substance abuse always brings risks with it, not just during pregnancy. However, it remains difficult to determine *if* a drug will have any effect on the developing fetus or how much of an effect it will have. This may depend on the amount used and the gestational period when it was used.

Many drugs affect the central nervous system. The central nervous system takes neural messages, triggered by sensory stimulation, to the brain to be interpreted. The brain then responds to the new information. For example, if a child runs out in front of someone's car, that visual stimulus must be transmitted to the brain via neurons. Once the brain has deciphered this new information, it sends a message to the body, again via neurons, telling it how to respond.

Drugs categorized as depressants slow down the transmission of neural messages. The depressants include legal drugs, such as alcohol and prescription pharmaceuticals like librium and valium, as well as illegal ones, such as quaaludes. The depressant most widely used during pregnancy is alcohol, no doubt in part because of its legality and availability. The effects of alcohol use on the fetus can be extensive.

The most preventable cause of congenital anomalies is maternal alcohol use. Alcohol is a potent teratogen, which crosses the placental membrane freely and can cause irreversible damage to the body and brain of the developing fetus. The United States Public Health Service has estimated that 86 percent of women drink at least once during pregnancy, with 20 to 25 percent drinking regularly. Further the Centers for Disease Control have estimated that more than 8,000 alcohol-damaged babies are born annually. Fetal alcohol exposure is the most commonly known cause of mental retardation. Exposure can be classified as Fetal Alcohol Effect (FAE) or Fetal Alcohol Syndrome (FAS). FAE involves slight to moderate damage, while FAS entails severe damage and developmental problems. The amount and type of

damage depends on the fetus's stage of development during exposure and the amount and frequency of alcohol consumption.
Decreased birth weight, prenatal growth retardation, small head
circumference, and heart defects are all characteristics of FAS.
Alcohol appears to be teratogenic only if used on specific days of
gestation.[2]

Other symptoms of FAS are facial deformities (such as ab-
normally slanted eyes), attention deficit disorder, learning
disabilities, low intelligence, and poor capacity for memoriza-
tion.[3] It is estimated that approximately one out of every 750
babies born each year has FAS; in fact, the figure is probably
higher. Like alcohol, most of the other depressants too can have
disastrous effects on the fetus if ingested by a woman at certain
times during her pregnancy.

As opposed to the depressants, which inhibit central nervous
system activity, stimulants excite central nervous system pro-
cessing. This can cause a tremendous strain on both the nervous
system and the body. Stimulants mimic the "fight or flight"
response the body naturally has when confronted with a fearful
situation. However, with stimulants this response usually has
a longer duration and occurs repeatedly (because the drug is
repeatedly used). Depending on the drug, the intensity of response could vary from mild to severe. Some stimulants, such
as caffeine, are considered relatively innocuous by the general
population, while others, such as cocaine, are perceived as dangerous. In terms of their effect on the developing fetus, however,
all stimulants should be viewed with caution.

Although more decaffeinated products are available now
than twenty years ago, caffeine is still consumed in vast quantities in coffee, tea, soft drinks, and chocolate. Like many drugs,
caffeine crosses the placenta. Research on the effects of caffeine
on a developing fetus has yielded mixed results. However, since

1980 the Food and Drug Administration (FDA) has *not* included caffeine on the list of compounds considered safe for use during pregnancy. The FDA indicated that research on animals suggests that caffeine causes birth defects, fetal death, and reduced birth weight.[4] More recently, researchers have found that moderate caffeine use does not increase the risk of spontaneous abortion, intrauterine growth retardation, or microencephaly.[5]

In any case there may be other reasons to give up caffeine during pregnancy.[6] Caffeine may sap calcium from the body and interfere with absorption of iron. In addition, products with caffeine often contain other products that can be detrimental to health, such as sugar. Finally, caffeine can cause temporary abnormal heartbeat, rapid respiration, and tremors in the newborn.[7] Some maternity packs provided to expectant mothers by obstetricians even include samples of decaffeinated coffee.

The verdict on caffeine may be somewhat tenuous, but abundant, unequivocal research demonstrates the harmful effects of smoking on a developing fetus. These effects are partially due to nicotine, a stimulant, but mainly due to the carcinogenic byproducts of smoke itself, such as carbon monoxide. If a woman smokes prior to her pregnancy but then gives it up, the fetus will not be affected, but if she continues to smoke, especially after the fourth month,[8] the chance of complications such as vaginal bleeding, miscarriage, abnormal placental implantation, premature placental detachment, premature ruptured membranes, and early delivery increases. It is possible that 14 percent of preterm deliveries in the United States are related to cigarette smoking.[9] Smoking also appears to be linked with low birth weights and an increased risk of sudden infant death syndrome (SIDS). Long-term effects may include physical and intellectual deficits in the child. Since the smoke crosses the placenta, limiting oxygen intake to the fetus, some of these effects may be related to oxygen deprivation. Not surprisingly, the risk increases with the dose. Secondhand smoke also poses a risk to the fetus. If a pregnant woman does not smoke but is frequently exposed to a smoke-filled environment at home or at work, the woman and the fetus may suffer passive damage from inhaling the sidestream smoke produced by burning cigarettes. In fact, in some cases the fetus may be as contaminated with smoke byproducts as if the pregnant woman herself had been smoking.

Since the 1980s the stimulant that has raised the most alarm, not just for pregnant women but for the general population, is cocaine and cocaine variants (crack). Crack is an affordable derivative of cocaine, which makes the drug more accessible to potential users, including pregnant women. It is estimated that one million women of childbearing age use cocaine. An infant that is born to a cocaine-abusing mother has an "increased risk of growth retardation *in utero,* increased incidence of premature rupture of membranes and labor, low birth weight and gestational size, poor brain growth, and increased possibility of brain infarction and hydrocephaly. Such newborns frequently manifest difficulty keeping food down; exhibit spasms, trembling and muscular rigidity; and resist cuddling by arching their backs." [10] Cocaine-exposed infants may also have difficulty bonding with their mother and have an increased risk for SIDS, respiratory problems, and eventual developmental delays. If the mother injected herself with cocaine products, the infant may have been exposed to HIV.

The third category of drugs are painkillers or narcotics. Painkillers range from over-the-counter medications such as acetaminophen to prescription medications such as codeine to illicit drugs such as heroin. Heroin, a derivative of opium, has received the most research attention. Pregnant women abusing heroin often give birth to infants who are born addicted and must undergo the ordeal of withdrawal.

Classically, withdrawal affects the central nervous system, gastrointestinal tract, and respiratory systems. The babies are highly
irritable, with tremors and hyperflexia and a shrill cry. Often
seizures accompany withdrawal. Again, these infants are hard to
console, and maternal bonding can be affected. Gastrointestinal
symptoms include vomiting and diarrhea, which can lead to
dehydration and electrolyte imbalance. . . . Long-term effects are
still unknown.[11]

Since heroin is generally injected, the addict is exposed to a
number of health risks that are in turn passed on to the fetus.
These include exposure to HIV and hepatitis. The fetus may
also be affected by the mother's poor health habits: malnutrition
and anemia are common among addicts.[12]

Lastly there are the hallucinogenic drugs, including marijuana, or cannabis sativa. Drugs in this category are primarily
used for recreational purposes and are mostly illegal. Unlike the
previous three categories, hallucinogens have a lower overall
potential for dependence or abuse.[13] Although smoking marijuana while pregnant does not seem to cause birth defects,
"Decreased birth weight and small size for gestational age are
markings of marijuana exposure. On the average the fetus is 3.5
ounces lighter than expected. Marijuana-withdrawing neonates
exhibit markedly decreased response to a light directed at their
eyes and significantly heightened tremors and startles. Long-
term effects are unknown."[14] Smoking marijuana does expose
the fetus to the carcinogenic byproducts of smoke. However,
since most marijuana users do not smoke every day or smoke
only a small amount per day, the fetus's exposure is significantly
less than that of a fetus whose mother smokes tobacco.

* * *

Many substance abusers abuse more than one substance. Pregnant women are no exception. A crack-addicted pregnant

woman is often addicted to alcohol, nicotine, and caffeine as well. This usually compounds the adverse effects on the fetus and makes treatment of both mother and child more difficult. Furthermore, addicts may not have the best health status prior to pregnancy, and their fetuses may suffer from the effects of little or no prenatal care. It is therefore difficult to determine which complications are directly due to substance abuse and which to associated behaviors and their health consequences.

It is also clear that substance abuse by the father can affect the health of the fetus and can have long-term effects on the eventual child. Cocaine apparently binds with the sperm but does not effect motility. Very little research focuses on the impact of paternal drug use on fetal health, and the results to date are meager and equivocal.

Legislation

In light of the potentially disastrous consequences, increased attention has been directed toward restricting pregnant women from using or abusing substances. This movement certainly contrasts with a general lack of societal and legislative efforts to secure safe and healthy environments for pregnant women and fetuses. Few federal or state regulations exist regarding VDTs (see chapter 4) or questionable reproductive technologies, and society is largely uninformed as to the potential risks related to these issues. But when regulation or censure is directed not toward corporations or the medical profession but toward individual women, legislative and societal response can be alarmingly swift. For example, in the latter part of the 1980s, the media began to heighten public awareness concerning the increase in crack-addicted pregnant women. By the end of the 1980s, substance-abusing pregnant women were being tried for numerous criminal and civil violations. Although the name of the offense may differ from case to case, the essence is always the same: behavior during pregnancy that creates risk or harm to the fetus.[15]

Sometimes prosecutors attempt to apply existing narcotics laws to pregnant women. In one of the most widely publicized cases, a Florida woman was found guilty of delivering a controlled substance to a minor. Jennifer Johnson used cocaine during two pregnancies, and both infants tested positive for cocaine. There were no signs of fetal distress in either case, but when the Department of Health and Rehabilitation Services learned of the positive test results, they decided to investigate and prosecute.

In Florida, as in most states, a fetus is not considered a person under the law. Therefore, while her children were still in utero, Johnson could not be found guilty of delivering a controlled substance to a minor (because they were technically not "people"). However, infants are considered persons, and the prosecutor argued that Johnson delivered a controlled substance to her children, via the umbilical cord, from the time the infants left the birth canal until the cord was clamped sixty to ninety seconds later. Johnson was convicted and sentenced to two hundred hours of community service, one year of "community control," and fourteen years of probation. During the first year she was to be subjected to random drug testing. She was also ordered to complete a drug rehabilitation program and to enter a judicially approved supervision program if any future pregnancies occurred.[16] Three years later, in 1992, her conviction was overturned by the Florida Supreme Court. Ironically, Johnson had sought treatment during her pregnancy but was refused because she was pregnant.

In other criminal cases, fetal abuse has been viewed as a form of child abuse, and women have been prosecuted under child protection laws. In a case that has parallels to the Johnson case, a prosecutor in Michigan charged Kimberly Hardy with delivering a controlled substance to a minor and second-degree child abuse. This prosecution was also unsuccessful.

Women have been charged with possession of a controlled substance, based on the presence of cocaine in their newborn, and with manslaughter. Most of the women who have been arrested for drug use during pregnancy have pleaded guilty. However, none of the women who contested have been convicted.[17] But most women cannot afford to appeal their convictions.

Substance-abusing women are also prosecuted under new laws that make drug use during pregnancy a crime in and of itself. These women are not arrested for selling or possessing illegal substances but simply for using drugs *while pregnant.* One proposed Ohio law mandated forced sterilization for women who could not overcome their addiction. Pete Wilson, the governor of California, proposed legislation that would make it a crime to give birth to an infant who was harmed by the mother's substance abuse (including alcohol abuse) or was addicted at birth.

Consider a possible parallel to this situation. What if Jon, an illegal substance abuser, went to a treatment center for help. He was not currently using drugs but clearly had a tendency toward physical and psychological addiction. Could the treatment center staff report Jon to authorities for previous illegal substance abuse and have him jailed? No, for Jon is not violating any laws unless he is in possession of the substance. However, Joann could be jailed, if she were pregnant and sought treatment. Why would the staff want to report her and possibly dissuade other addicts from seeking help? Some states have informant laws that "deputize" health care workers and require them to report instances of substance-abusing pregnant women. In this situation health care workers are faced with a catch-22. Report the woman, thus violating physician-patient confidentiality and possibly frightening other substance abusers away from treatment, or fail to report her, and risk being held in contempt of court or found guilty of a criminal violation. The American Medical Association and the American Public Health Association have already voiced their opposition to the efforts of the "pregnancy police."

Another method used to incarcerate pregnant substance abusers is to sentence them to jail when they are convicted of another crime that would generally warrant probation. This type of conviction provides very little recourse.

The Constitution guarantees all individuals the right to equal protection under the law, which means, among other things, that the law applies equally to all citizens. For example, the Constitution would prohibit the enacting of a law that criminalized a behavior *only if* the actor were of a certain race. Similarly, no law may be enacted that only males or only females could conceivably violate. Since men cannot gestate a child, they could never violate a law that criminalizes a behavior only when the actor is pregnant. Any such law would seemingly be unconstitutional.

Consider a Susan Doe. The day before her child was born, she used cocaine. Her infant tests positive for cocaine but is healthy and shows no sign of addiction or impairment. Susan is nevertheless convicted of child abuse and sentenced to jail. At the same time another woman, Julie Doe, gets pregnant and leads a model lifestyle throughout her entire pregnancy. She receives excellent prenatal care and eliminates all potentially harmful substances from her diet. However, the day before Julie is to deliver, she has a fight with her estranged husband, Tom, and he batters her, endangering the fetus. The infant is unharmed, but Tom's actions could have resulted in serious consequences for the child. Because the fetus is not considered a person in most states, Tom would probably not be found guilty of any crime except battery of Julie, even though he should also be convicted of child abuse, as Susan was. If the fetus is considered a person in Susan's case, it should also be considered a person in Tom's. Yet few courts are clamoring to bring child abuse charges against batterers and balance this disparity. Making an action illegal only when the actor is pregnant targets one group in a discriminatory way.

These laws also discriminate against women of low socioeconomic status and women of color, who are disproportionately represented in arrests and prosecutions. This disproportion probably stems in part from the fact that these women are more likely to come to the attention of state-operated or public agencies.

Reinterpreting laws to create a crime where none previously existed also raises serious questions of due process. Assume that a state has no law criminalizing drug use by pregnant women. Furthermore, in that state the fetus is not considered a person. But a prosecutor, seeking to convict a drug-addicted mother who has just given birth, attempts to apply to newborns the existing laws against delivering controlled substances to a minor (using the umbilical cord theory). How can the woman be held responsible for violating a law that, so far as she knew or could have known, did not exist? How could anyone possibly be required to know or imagine all the possible *permutations* of a law that might expose them to prosecution? Laws are precisely formulated so that citizens know what they can and cannot do and prosecutors know what they can and cannot prosecute. Legislative bodies make laws; prosecutors are not supposed to construct them ad hoc, inventing interpretations that will serve their own agendas.

Criminalizing drug use during pregnancy may also violate the right to privacy, including the right to bodily integrity, the right to autonomy in reproductive choices, and the right to confidential patient-physician relationships. In short, these laws threaten procreative choice altogether. Pregnancy also creates a unique situation in the application of law. For example, can a woman be found guilty of violating a law against abusing substances while pregnant if she did not know she was pregnant when she abused the substances? Such a scenario highlights one of the myriad of problems with legislating against substance abuse while pregnant.

In general, legal standards for criminal convictions are more stringent than those for civil sanctions. Criminal convictions of pregnant substance abusers are usually reversed on appeal, but civil penalties are more likely to be upheld. For example, the Department of Family Services can be called in to institute civil proceedings for child abuse against a pregnant substance abuser, and she can be penalized with less chance of reversal than with a criminal conviction. She may not be incarcerated, but she may well lose custody of her child(ren).

Like criminal statutes, civil child abuse and neglect statutes were never meant to apply to prenatal behavior. However, when these statutes are reinterpreted the fetus is often afforded the rights of a person. Sometimes prenatal substance abuse is presumed to be evidence that future mistreatment of the child will occur, and temporary or permanent placement in foster care is sought.

A well-publicized civil proceeding took place in 1992 in Connecticut.[18] The defendant, Jean, received little prenatal care and abused drugs during her pregnancy. Jean gave birth to Valerie, who had symptoms of prenatal exposure to cocaine. The Department of Child and Youth Services filed petitions for temporary and permanent custody that, if approved, would have terminated parental rights, based on Jean's (and her husband's) prenatal conduct. The trial and appellate courts terminated all parental rights. However, the Supreme Court of Connecticut reversed this decision, on the grounds that the statutory provisions permitting termination of parental rights were not meant to apply to prenatal conduct. Other state supreme courts have reached the opposite conclusion on this issue.

Through civil proceedings, it also becomes possible to "incarcerate" a pregnant substance abuser without criminal charges. If the woman presents a danger to herself or others, she can be civilly committed to an institution until she is no longer a threat. Loosely interpreted, this means that her drug abuse poses a threat to the fetus, the status of which has been elevated to personhood. If commitment is shrewdly timed, the woman will give birth before she is released and the courts can then take custody of the newborn while she is institutionalized.

Regardless of whether the proceedings are criminal or civil, in order for them to hold up on appeal, they must not violate constitutional fundamental rights. So far, this issue has not been debated in the federal courts.

Forced Medical Interventions

Legal protection of "fetal rights" at the expense of maternal rights has already extended to forced medical interventions. One of the *least* intrusive of these procedures involves mandatory drug testing of pregnant women. Some physicians will only provide obstetric care if the patient agrees to random drug and HIV testing. In fact, the federal government, which on the whole has demonstrated a tremendous lack of concern for the health of women or fetuses, has recently urged physicians to counsel pregnant women to be tested for HIV.

On the more intrusive extreme, women have been compelled

to undergo cesarean sections or blood transfusions against their will in order to save the lives of their fetuses. In these cases, the court found that the state's interest in protecting the potential life of the fetus outweighed the woman's rights. The court's authority was even further extended in *In re Dubreuil.*

> In *Dubreuil,* a pregnant woman had suffered complications following her child's Caesarean section delivery. Although she needed blood transfusions to remain alive, she refused the transfusions for religious reasons. . . . What was unusual about the case was that the child had already been born. The court noted the woman's four young children, including the newborn, would be abandoned if she died, and it was mostly for the children's benefit that the court forced the woman to undergo the life-saving procedure.[19]

Although some courts have declined to compel women to undergo procedures against their will, the majority of jurisdictions seem to favor forced intervention.[20] Given the emergency nature of these decisions, it is often moot for the woman to appeal, because the procedure has already been performed.

Advances in medical technology have made it possible to perform surgery on a fetus to correct deformities and birth defects. It is not only possible but feasible that courts could one day compel pregnant women to undergo fetal surgery. This precedent could be even further extended to require not only lifesaving fetal surgery but therapeutic fetal surgery as well. Unlike lifesaving surgery, therapeutic surgery is designed to enhance the quality of the child's life—at the expense, if necessary, of the mother's privacy rights.

One scholar has even contemplated the possibility that a biological father may at some point be able to compel a biological mother to undergo fetal surgery.[21] Such a development may seem unrealistic, but existing law lays the foundation for it.

Although the Supreme Court has never upheld laws that require a biological father's consent before a woman can obtain an abortion, recently these laws have been *very* narrowly defeated. Second, after the child is born, fathers theoretically have equal rights with mothers. For example, it is difficult for a woman to place her child for adoption without the biological father's consent. Finally, after a child is born the father has ongoing legal rights and responsibilities, such as child support. Given that a father may have a greater financial and emotional burden if a child is born with deficits, a court might find that he had the right to force the mother to have fetal surgery.

Perhaps the most disturbing aspect of the recent trend toward incarcerating or prosecuting pregnant substance abusers is the "slippery slope" effect. It is difficult to determine, or even imagine, what may or may not be defined as substance abuse in the future. Already Pete Wilson (as well as many others) has proposed that alcohol be included. Other legal substances that could represent threats to the fetus, including cigarettes and caffeine, might also be subject to legislation. If the goal is to control the amount of exposure the fetus has to potentially hazardous conditions, any number of behaviors may ultimately need to be regulated, including the amount of prenatal care. However, it is unclear who would pay for prescribed increases in prenatal care if the mothers themselves were not able to do so. Exposure to work stress and toxins may also need to be controlled, which would be difficult to balance with the decision the Supreme Court reached in *Johnson Controls* (see chapter 4), that women should not be disparately treated in the workplace due to their status. It may one day be possible to force pregnant women to undergo amniocentesis to detect genetic and birth "defects." Who will determine what action is to be taken when there are positive results—legislatures or parents? (And if parents, which one?)

Laws that lead to the incarceration or prosecution of pregnant substance abusers can also have unintended but devastating practical consequences. Most importantly, pregnant substance abusers are very often deterred from obtaining prenatal care because they fear incarceration. In addition to the fact that incarceration itself is unpleasant, many of these women fear that they could be forced to "involuntarily abandon" their other children. Fear of losing custody of children is the primary reason substance-abusing pregnant women do not seek treatment. When mothers are incarcerated, their children are often placed in foster care. Once foster placement has occurred and the mother is saddled with a criminal record, it may be difficult to regain custody. Of course, proponents of incarcerating substance-abusing pregnant women argue that foster care is a healthier option for these children. However, there are already a tremendous number of children in foster care or waiting to be placed in foster care. Recall that the shortage of foster care placement led House Speaker Newt Gingrich to suggest in 1994 the revival of the orphanage.

Moreover, incarceration of the mother may be unhealthy for the fetus, for the mother endures not only the stress of arrest and prosecution but the hazards and deprivations of prison life.

There is substantial evidence of harassment and mistreatment of women [prisoners] explicitly because they are pregnant. . . . One report cited a pattern of assigning pregnant women to work requiring a great deal of exertion and heavy lifting, even when the women had a history of miscarriage. Sometimes needed medical care is delayed, resulting in miscarriages and babies born dead, or who die shortly after birth. Inmates have charged that such delay is often deliberate.

Several class actions have been filed charging systematic deficiencies in prenatal care provided to incarcerated pregnant women. *Yeager v. Smith* alleged violations of the Eighth and Fourteenth Amendment rights of pregnant women in the Kern county jail and work camp. Of eight plaintiffs, three had miscarriages and one gave birth lying on a mat in the jail hallway. The child died shortly thereafter. The remaining four plaintiffs were, at the time of filing, exposed to hepatitis and measles and were denied vitamins, exercise and needed medical care for serious conditions that threatened their pregnancies.[22]

Pregnant inmates are seldom provided with less restrictive maternity clothes and often must wear belly chains, restraints that strap around the waist, or chains that extend to the ankles and/or wrists. Some prison programs directed toward assisting pregnant women with substance abuse have been successful, but most prisons do not have such programs.

Some states have recognized that incarceration of pregnant women may not be in the best interests of the fetus, the mother, or the state. Laws that allow judges to delay incarceration of pregnant women convicted of nonviolent crimes until six weeks after the birth of the child or the termination of the pregnancy have been approved in several states. This alternative provides the mother an opportunity to bond with the infant and to secure living arrangements for the child during her incarceration, thus saving the state health care and placement expenditures.

Attempts to incarcerate pregnant substance abusers in order to benefit the fetus are ineffectual for a number of reasons. For example, by the time most women can be incarcerated, they have passed their first trimester, which is usually the period during which the fetus is most vulnerable to harmful substances. Moreover, drugs are often obtainable in prison.

Ultimately these laws are illogical and unproductive. They don't deter women from abusing substances, only from seeking treatment. Far from ensuring proper care, the laws often act as an obstacle to care. It would make more sense to offer pregnant women who seek assistance with substance abuse prosecutorial immunity than to attempt to sanction them.[23] Moreover, removing a child from parents after delivery does not prevent prenatal injury.

Prevention

Although the drugs of choice at any given moment may be new, the problem of substance abuse is very old. Substance abuse has traditionally been considered more of a man's than a woman's problem. This perception is partially based in reality and partially in gender stereotypes. After all, abusing substances is very "unladylike" behavior. Consequently, women substance abusers have generally been overlooked by society, researchers, and treatment programs. In comparison to male substance abusers, female substance abusers get little research attention and pregnant substance abusers even less.

Correspondingly, most treatment programs were designed with male substance abusers (often criminals) in mind. Therapists are trained in techniques that may be nonproductive or counterproductive with female substance abusers. Therapy strategies are short-term and confrontational in nature. These strategies would not work with typical female substance abusers.

> Over 80% have histories of parental substance abuse, child physical abuse, or sexual abuse. Additionally, the women report that very few of the general or mental health care professionals who have treated them have inquired about their childhood experiences. Our staff has found that these underlying issues can seriously complicate efforts to help these women become drug-free, nurturing parents.
>
> Individuals with abusive backgrounds tend to have low self-esteem, which, in turn, negatively influences their educational achievements and interferes with the development of healthy social networks.[24]

Given this profile, women substance abusers would probably benefit from long-term therapy with a more humanistic and less confrontational approach.

If it is difficult to find a treatment program geared toward women, it is virtually impossible to find one that accepts pregnant substance abusers. Dr. Wendy Chavkin (1989) surveyed 95 percent of the drug treatment programs in New York City and found that 54 percent of them excluded pregnant women. In addition, 67 percent denied treatment to pregnant addicts on Medicaid, and 87 percent denied treatment to pregnant crack addicts.[25]

Pregnant substance abusers represent new challenges to treatment programs. For example, detoxification may be difficult or impossible with pregnant women, depending on the drug used and the stage of the pregnancy. The stresses of drug withdrawal may harm the fetus or terminate the pregnancy. Additionally, the staff must be trained and the facilities equipped to handle prenatal issues and emergencies. As is true of many women, pregnant women may have other children whom they cannot abandon in order to attend an inpatient drug rehabilitation program, so child care facilities must also be available. Finally, therapists must take into account that the woman may be in treatment over the protests of an abusive, often addicted, partner.

An effective drug prevention program for women would have all of the following additional components: advocates who will assist with other agencies, educational and career services, aftercare, assistance with basic needs such as housing, multiple counseling modalities, and multiple types of services (i.e., ranging from inpatient to home-based).[26]

The number of treatment programs that accept pregnant women is unlikely to increase. Basically, treating pregnant substance abusers requires treatment centers to invest money to modify their programs while simultaneously increasing their liability, all for little profit potential. Pregnant substance abusers are a higher-risk population than substance abusers in general, due to pregnancy-induced health issues. Furthermore, proportionally few of the clients presenting to private facilities will be pregnant and substance abusing. Federal or state-funded clinics are more likely to see pregnant substance abusers, because many of them are either on Medicaid or have no insurance at all.

Moreover societal and legislative response is presently geared more toward punishment than prevention. Although many individuals view substance abuse as a disease, if the abuser is a pregnant woman, a moralistic tone creeps in and the woman is seen as a "bad mother" who willfully indulged herself at the expense of her child's health. In 1992, of the $12 billion allocated by the federal government to drug programs, less than 20 percent was spent on prevention and treatment:[27] "The federal budget for the fiscal year 1992 proposed an allocation of $331,169,000 to construct and fund 3,600 new prison beds, and $99,000,000 to fund 8,997 new drug treatment slots. Note that prison beds are much more expensive than drug treatment slots: One prison bed costs $91,991 as compared to $11,004 per drug treatment slot."[28]

This emphasis on incarceration instead of prevention and rehabilitation is extremely shortsighted given the cost to society from babies born drug addicted. Although prevention would entail a greater "front-end" investment, the long-term expenditure would be greatly diminished. In 1992, the cost of treating drug-exposed infants was estimated at $3 billion.[29] This does not include the costs of the longer postnatal care required by drug-addicted mothers, the expense of foster care or special education programs, or the eventual costs to society from lost wages, lifetime care (for some), or crime (committed by the mother or the child). This figure also does not include the cost of maintaining "boarder babies," those who are abandoned by their mothers and because of addictions or physical deficits must remain in the hospital. Some of these babies are HIV-positive. When prevention programs have been implemented, they have generally saved government monies and been successful. In fact, for every dollar invested in drug treatment, society saves five dollars in reduced crime and welfare costs.[30]

Although tremendous societal anger is directed at women who continue to use substances while pregnant, few alternatives are available to them. If they go to a federally funded clinic they cannot get a federally funded abortion. Often, by the time they learn they are pregnant, it may be too late for an abortion. If they seek prenatal care, the word on the street is that they will be incarcerated and lose custody of their other children. Even if all these obstacles are surmounted, there are probably not appropriate treatment facilities available and if they are, they often have long waiting lists.

Legislation against substance abuse during pregnancy is clearly not the solution. This approach has no tangible benefits and infringes on constitutional rights. To grant the fetus the same rights as the mother (or even greater rights) is to take a step back toward paternalistic protection of women and fetuses by the legislature and legal systems. If women will ultimately have the responsibility for the children they bear, they should also be responsible for choices related to their own prenatal care.

It is an odd coincidence that debates over the status of the fetus arise at a time when the validity of *Roe v. Wade* is increasingly under attack. If the fetus is elevated to a person in the context of substance abuse, then the foundation of *Roe v. Wade* may be jeopardized (see chapter 5). Maybe it is no coincidence after all.

[4]

Politics and Reproductive Issues in the Workplace

ॐ

*T*he politics of reproduction and the family were showcased in the 1992 presidential election. Pivotal campaign issues focused on the reproductive rights of women and support for the family, particularly in the workplace. George Bush was criticized for paying lip service to "family values" while stifling legislation, such as the Family Leave Act, that might have assisted families in their attempt to balance work and home life.

This disparity should not have come as a surprise to women, who have long been familiar with workplace discrimination revolving around family and reproductive issues. Many women have found themselves inappropriately terminated from jobs as the result of a pregnancy or denied promotion (or even employment) due to potential future pregnancies. A legal remedy, albeit burdensome, has been provided for such discrimination. However, sometimes even the courts have difficulty understanding and identifying discrimination when it is interwoven with reproductive rights.

For example, in 1990, the Supreme Court heard arguments in the case of *International Union, United Automobile, Aerospace and Agricultural Implement Workers of America, UAW, et al. v. Johnson Controls, Inc.*[1] (hereinafter referred to as *Johnson Controls*). The plaintiffs appealed to the Supreme Court after both lower courts had ruled in favor of the defendant, Johnson Controls, Inc.

Johnson Controls, Inc., used lead when manufacturing batteries. Initially, the company did not exclude pregnant women or women capable of childbearing from positions requiring exposure to lead but strongly discouraged women from taking these positions and had them sign a form, presumably serving as a liability waiver, indicating that they had been advised of the risks. However, in 1982, Johnson Controls, Inc. implemented a new policy, known as a fetal protection policy. Now, all women who were pregnant, or merely capable of childbearing, would be excluded from jobs that could expose them to lead. The purported goal of the policy was to protect unborn children from risks associated with maternal exposure to lead. However, unless a woman could medically document her inability to bear children, she was excluded from any position that entailed exposure to lead, whether or not she ever intended to become pregnant. This policy not only limited women's exposure to lead but also to higher-paying positions.

The plaintiffs in this class action suit argued that the fetal protection policy at Johnson Controls, Inc., constituted sexual discrimination. One plaintiff had chosen to be sterilized to avoid losing her job. A second plaintiff suffered a wage reduction when she was transferred out of a job that exposed her to lead. Conversely, a male plaintiff, who was planning to start a family, requested a leave of absence in order to lower his lead exposure and was denied. The Supreme Court held that the policy was discriminatory and violated both the Civil Rights Act of 1964[2] and Title VII as amended by the Pregnancy Discrimination Act.[3] The latter act states that decisions about the welfare of potential children should be left to the prospective parents, not the prospective parents' employer.

Governmental agencies such as the National Institute of Occupational Safety and Health (NIOSH) were designed to protect the health of all employees. Their failure to set specific guidelines encouraged Johnson Controls, Inc., and many other corporations to develop their own policies, perhaps attempting to limit liability. Employees could not make decisions for themselves regarding exposure to reproductive hazards, because employers made this decision for them. As a "bonus," fetal protection policies could also provide a way to prevent the hiring and promotion of women while bearing the appearance of a humanistic concern for the safety of employees and their potential offspring.

Two factors suggest that the fetal protection policy was simply a vehicle for discrimination. First, as the court recognized, the male reproductive system, like the female, can be adversely impacted by exposure to toxins. If so, why expose either women or men to these toxins? Transferring women from these positions forces men to work in an unhealthy environment. Instead of transferring employees, the risk should be eliminated.

More importantly, in occupations where women workers predominate, such as dry cleaning or hair styling, women are not transferred out of positions that expose them to potential reproductive hazards. Concern for women and/or the fetus does not appear to come into play until men and women are competing for the same position. When the population exposed to potential reproductive hazards is almost exclusively female, the danger is minimized or not investigated. A glaring example of this minimization is the use of computer monitors or video display terminals (VDTs) in the workplace. The impact of patriarchal society on reproductive issues in the workplace is clearly reflected in this issue.

The Computer Age

The link between electromagnetic emissions (such as those from VDTs) and health hazards has recently become the subject of increased attention. Power lines and cellular phones have been investigated in relation to increased cancer rates. The concern over emissions does not focus on periodic exposure, for example, from using hair dryers, but rather on prolonged exposure such as occurs with VDT usage. A connection between the use of VDTs and reproductive complications was first suspected in the late 1970s, when clusters of women VDT operators began reporting higher than average rates of miscarriage. The reports are too numerous to mention but consider the following examples:

In late 1979 and early 1980, six out of 10 pregnant women who worked at Sears Roebuck's Southwest Regional Office in Dallas "had experienced spontaneous abortions, and another employee had delivered a premature infant who subsequently died. Upon investigating, CDC Centers for Disease Control officials determined that eight out of twelve pregnancies over a fourteen-month period of women working in Department 168 of the Sears office—a large room containing 25 VDTs in one corner—had ended either in miscarriage or neonatal death."[4]

In 1979, four out of seven pregnant VDT operators who worked in the classified advertising department of the *Toronto Star* gave birth to infants with defects: "One baby was born with a club-foot; another with a cleft palate; a third with an underdeveloped eye; and the fourth with multiple heart abnormalities." All of these babies were born within a two-month period to young women who had neither smoked nor taken drugs during their pregnancies. During that same time period, three employees at the *Star* who didn't work on VDTs gave birth to normal babies.[5]

Between 1979 and 1984, 24 out of 48 pregnancies among VDT operators at the United Airlines reservation centers in San Francisco "resulted in miscarriages, birth defects, neonatal deaths, premature births, and other abnormal outcomes."[6]

More than fifteen years have elapsed since these reports were publicized and a possible relationship between VDTs and reproduction complications was first theorized. During that time period, very little research on this issue has been conducted, especially in the United States, and the research findings that have been published have been contradictory.

Just When You Thought It Was Safe

The focus of research on VDTs and reproductive complications is electromagnetic emissions. Electrical appliances emit electromagnetic radiation when activated. Natural sources of electricity, such as lightning, also emit electromagnetic radiation. "Electromagnetic" implies two fields, an electric or electronic field and a magnetic field. In VDTs, an electronic beam passes through a cathode ray tube (CRT), activating phosphors that coat the inside of the tube. This activation of phosphors emits radiation, and the radiation creates the light that allows colors and images to be projected on the computer monitor. The radiation emitted falls into two frequency ranges; very low frequency radiation (VLF) and extremely low frequency radiation (ELF). It is unclear which is more dangerous to consumers. Researchers have generally focused on the effects of VLF radiation on spontaneous abortions or miscarriages, neglecting the effect of ELF radiation, which some believe is more dangerous. Early research was methodologically flawed and was conducted on now out dated computer monitors.[7] Most recent research is not substantially better.

One of the initial studies in the United States was conducted at the Northern California Kaiser-Permanente Medical Care Program.[8] Women who had received pregnancy tests at the Kaiser-Permanente health maintenance organization between 15 September 1981 and 30 June 1982 were recruited to participate in the study. The original purpose of the study was not to investigate the effect of VDT exposure on pregnancy but rather to study the effect on pregnancy of a pesticide spray used in California. Goldhaber and her colleagues then embedded exposure to other environmental factors, including VDTs, within the design. The pregnancy outcome of 1,583 women was examined, largely through participant questionnaire responses and review of medical records. The researchers found an elevated risk of miscarriage (often considered an indicator of abnormality in pregnancy), but not birth defects, for women who reported using VDTs more than twenty hours per week during their first trimester of pregnancy. Unfortunately, like most of the research reviewed here, this study was conducted years after the fact, when recall could be faulty.

In the same year Goldhaber and her colleagues published their findings, 1988, Finnish researchers published conflicting findings.[9] Nurminen and Kurppa found that VDT users demonstrated no increased risk of spontaneous abortion and no differences in length of gestation or birth weight of infants. However, Nurminen and Kurppa did not actually measure VDT exposure but merely assessed probable exposure by asking women their job titles and having them describe an ordinary work day. Purporting to study VDT exposure without asking any questions about actual VDT usage is akin to studying the effects of smoking on health without asking participants about their smoking habits.

Since 1988, research results have continued to be confusing and contradictory. Bryant and Love[10] conducted interviews of 334 women who had spontaneously aborted and concluded that VDT usage was not a factor. In contrast, Windham and her colleagues[11] found that the risk of intrauterine growth retardation was slightly higher with greater VDT usage. They suggested that the effects of VDT use may vary according to gestational stage at which the mother is exposed, with earlier exposure (twelve weeks or less) resulting in a greater impact on pregnancy. (Pregnancies are generally more vulnerable in the early stages.) If this speculation is correct, it is possible that many women may be unknowingly having spontaneous abortions due to VDT exposure before they are even aware that they are pregnant. Obviously, it would be very difficult for researchers to safely measure this impact.

Other researchers have suggested that VDTs do not increase reproductive complications. In a pair of studies, Brandt and Nielsen[12] and Nielsen and Brandt[13] reported no increased risk of congenital malformations or spontaneous abortions among VDT operators. Another study (Roman et al.) confirmed these findings as regards spontaneous abortions.[14]

In this myriad of research results, two studies warrant discussion in greater detail, the first because it brings to the fore how political pressures influence the investigation of reproductive issues in the workplace. In 1991, NIOSH reported the results of a long-anticipated study of the contribution of VDTs to reproductive complications.[15] NIOSH investigators originally proposed a study that would allow for investigation into a number of factors affecting VDT operators, such as stress, in addition to electromagnetic emissions. NIOSH also planned to examine the possible connection between VDT use and birth defects and infertility. The proposed study would have been the most detailed and comprehensive research project on VDTs ever implemented.

Bell South Corporation was to provide the participants. However, after consultants for Bell South reviewed the NIOSH proposal, Bell South objected to the proposed inclusion of questions on stress and fertility, which they said were "intrusive" and "irrelevant" (and no doubt posed significant liability issues). Bell South Corporation appealed to the Office of Management and Budget (OMB) to intercede. The Office of Management and Budget was granted authority to review the study under the infamous Paperwork Reduction Act. At that time the OMB operated under the auspices of the Reagan administration and had been accused of obstructing research on environmental and occupational hazards, especially if the research touched on reproductive issues. (Later an independent review team substantiated this claim.) So it did not come as a surprise when the OMB decreed that 90 percent of the questions, primarily those on stress and fertility, be eliminated from the questionnaire.[16] Additionally, the OMB indicated that if NIOSH still found a difference between pregnant women exposed to VDTs and pregnant women not exposed to VDTs, they would be required to validate these outcomes through a review of medical records.[17] Finally, after deleting the core of the study, the OMB approved the remainder in 1986.

Teresa Schnorr and her colleagues conducted the truncated NIOSH study. Directory-assistance operators who used VDTs were compared with general assistance operators who used a low-radiation, light-emitting diode (LED) screen rather than a VDT. The research team interviewed women who had been pregnant, married, between eighteen and thirty-three years old, and employed full-time for *as little as one day* as a directory-assistance or general operator between 1 January 1983 and 1 August 1986. To qualify as data for the study, their pregnancies must have ended in a spontaneous abortion, live birth, or stillbirth during this time period. Women fitting these criteria were interviewed for twenty-five minutes sometime between July 1987 and August 1988. Therefore, at best, women were interviewed about their pregnancy and exposure at least one year after the fact; at worst, five and a half years after. Moreover, emissions were not measured until 1990, four to seven years after these women had been exposed to the VDT. Furthermore, only two models of VDTs had been used, so only the effect of these two models could be measured. As a result, sixty-seven miscarriages were not included in the study because the women were no longer working at one of these two models at the time of the miscarriage.[18] Finally, it should be noted that all women had been exposed to some background level of ELF radiation, presumably a high level, at the phone company.

Not surprisingly, this group of researchers did not find an increased rate of spontaneous abortion among VDT operators. Since the effects of VDT exposure on fertility, congenital malformations, birth weight, or premature birth were not examined, no conclusions could be drawn related to these issues. Despite all of these limitations, this study was hailed as a success; it was published in the *New England Journal of Medicine,* and every major newspaper carried an account of the findings (generally under a headline proclaiming the ensured safety of VDTs).

Contrast the NIOSH study, and the subsequent glorification of its results, with a Finnish study published a year later.[19] The Finnish study was as well designed as the NIOSH study, perhaps better, yet the results went virtually unnoticed by the press.

The Finnish researchers examined the pregnancy outcome of women employed as bank clerks and clerical workers in Finland. Information regarding health history, work tasks, and the use of VDTs during the first trimester of pregnancy was obtained from participants and their employers. The researchers also obtained twelve emissions measures from the VDTs, including both VLF and ELF emissions. Recall that, previously, researchers had focused primarily on VLF emissions.

Like NIOSH, the Finnish researchers obtained information retrospectively. However, they tested seventeen models of VDTs. Like NIOSH, the Finnish researchers did not find an increased risk of spontaneous abortion relating to VLF emissions. However, when a high level of ELF emissions was recorded, the risk of spontaneous abortion was three and a half times greater for VDT operators. This relationship was still significant after the effects of ergonomic factors and job characteristics were removed. Unlike the NIOSH study, the Finnish research received little acclaim.

The one thing all researchers, including those involved in the NIOSH study, agree upon is that more research needs to be conducted. The numerous flaws in all the previous research designs make any conclusions questionable. For example, none of the studies was designed with a prospective focus, enabling researchers to examine the outcome of pregnancies as they occur as opposed to retrospectively.[20] Researchers have relied on the recall of sometimes remote events, providing participants with an opportunity to color their memories. A prospective study would provide an opportunity for emissions to be measured *during* pregnancy, instead of having to rely on biased memories regarding emissions, work stress, or ergonomics. Information about the strength of the emission and the duration of exposure could then be combined to provide an exposure index. However, ethical considerations would probably prohibit a prospective study, given the detrimental effects stress could have on participants and their fetuses.

In addition to not thoroughly exploring the effect of VDT

emissions on reproduction, researchers have neglected numerous other factors. For example, no one has investigated whether VDT exposure affects male or female fertility. This is an important consideration given the purported recent rise in unexplained infertility. The cumulative effect of VDT exposure might account for some cases of temporary, or even permanent, infertility.

Furthermore, the effects of stress or ergonomic factors in combination with emissions have been virtually ignored. Nor has anyone examined whether stress or poor ergonomics could lead to or aggravate reproductive complications irrespective of emissions. The causes of stress among VDT operators are also unclear, as is the relationship between repetitive strain injuries and reproductive complications.

At a time when medical technology is rapidly advancing, particularly in the area of reproduction, why has it been so difficult to design or implement a relatively definitive study on VDTs and reproductive complications? Undeniably, it is difficult to control the many factors that might send data askew, for example, maternal health histories. Clearly it would be unethical to select a relatively homogeneous group of pregnant women and randomly assign one-fourth of them to high electromagnetic exposure, one-fourth to moderate exposure, one-fourth to low exposure, and one-fourth to no exposure and then measure the rate of reproductive complications. However, most studies completed to date lack even the basics of sound research methodology. It almost appears that scientists are avoiding definitive research in this area. If a relationship between reproductive complications and VDTs was discovered, strict regulation, perhaps legislation, would be required to ensure a safe work environment for VDT operators. However, partly due to lack of research support, several progressive attempts at legislation have already failed.

Attempts to Legislate/Regulate

Numerous bills have been introduced, ordinances proposed, and guidelines recommended over the last fifteen years in an effort to protect VDT operators from various associated health risks.[21] Most of these endeavors focus on safeguards against the physical effects of prolonged VDT usage, such as eye strain or muscular problems. Some include modifications of workplace practices or of workstations. Others include recommendations for pregnant VDT operators. However, despite a number of attempts, only one ordinance regulating safety standards has actually been approved, and then only temporarily.

In December 1990, San Francisco approved a union-backed ordinance regulating most workplaces with VDTs. The ordinance required employers with more than fifteen employees (including the city government) to provide regular breaks, adjustable workstations, and training on safe VDT usage. Primarily, the ordinance was designed to prevent repetitive strain injuries, such as carpal tunnel syndrome. Not surprisingly, the ordinance met with opposition from members of the business community.

Originally, plans to limit electromagnetic radiation exposure were included in the ordinance. However, in a compromise with the business community, these plans were scrapped, and an advisory committee was established, purportedly to monitor research published on the effects of radiation from VDTs on operators. The ordinance did include recommendations suggesting that pregnant women be allowed to transfer to non-VDT work should they desire to do so. Businesses were given two years in which to comply with all the provisions of the ordinance, and compliance was to be monitored by the San Francisco Health Department. In 1992, however, a judge struck down the ordinance, asserting that individual cities did not have the authority to regulate safety in the workplace.[22] The judge indicated that legislation regulating the workplace was under federal and state jurisdiction. Interestingly, the federal government was joined by a major computer manufacturer in challenging the ordinance in the first place. Another attempt at legislation, in Suffolk County, New York, similarly failed, because the court ruled that the county did not have the authority to legislate.

Unfortunately, even when bills regarding VDTs and employee safety do come before state legislatures, they suffer similar fates. For example, a bill presented to the Massachusetts House Commerce and Labor Committee required employers to provide VDT operators with non-VDT work or radiation-free equipment during pregnancy. Action on the bill was delayed pending the publication of studies on the health effects of VDTs. This could be a long wait. Moreover, even with health hazards such as repetitive strain injuries, which are well documented and cost employers an estimated $100 billion annually in claims, legislation is still stonewalled, as it was in San Francisco and Suffolk County. In fact, in 1995, the Occupational Safety and Health Administration (OSHA) yielded to political pressure from some members of the House of Representatives and rescinded plans to issue regulations protecting workers from repetitive strain injuries.

Previous bills introduced into the Massachusetts legislature were also thwarted. One legislative member indicated that these bills simply became obsolete, because technological changes have now made it possible to design a more ergonomically efficient workstation. Apparently this member did not consider the possibility that employers would not upgrade their workstations unless compelled to by law. Eventually, the Massachusetts bill died from lack of interest.

Maine and Rhode Island have managed to secure statutes

that require better instruction of employees on the safe use of VDTs. In Rhode Island, the Department of Labor was required to develop an "informational brochure relating to the use of video display terminals in the workplace."[23] The statute also required that the Department of Labor, in conjunction with business, industry, and labor develop a plan for disseminating the brochure to all "concerned parties" and for providing a series of training programs and seminars expanding on information in the brochure.

In Maine, employers are required to provide an education and training program to describe both proper use of VDTs and protective measures operators can take to avoid injury.[24] Employers must also instruct employees on the use of ergonomic equipment and healthy posture. Finally, employers are required to notify employees of their rights to such education and training. All of these provisions must be carried out within one month of employment.

Both the Rhode Island and Maine statutes are relatively obscure and have received little attention. The impact of the statutes or the degree of compliance is unknown. In 1994, Connecticut approved a statute that required the commissioners of Labor and Health Services to establish guidelines regarding safety standards for state employees who use VDTs by 1 July 1994.[25] Since these guidelines do not apply to private industry, they may not meet with ardent opposition.

Businesses as well as communities have presented strong opposition to legislation regulating potential workplace hazards. In fact, businesses, including, of course, the computer industry, have reportedly spent millions to squelch interest and concern.[26] Communities often fear that the possible additional expense of implementing safety regulations will deter businesses from locating in their area or even provoke some businesses into leaving. This is a realistic concern[27] and supports the need for federal regulation. Unfortunately, the House Appropriations Subcommittee slashed funding for NIOSH, the federal agency designed to advocate for workplace safety, 24.9 percent for the 1996 fiscal year. Similar proposals to reduce the OSHA budget have been advanced.

Conversely, legislation to protect workers from the hazards of VDTs has few powerful proponents. Politicians generally avoid this issue, undoubtedly because of the potential backlash from business and industry. VDT operators do not have their own union. However, some unions that include clerical workers have advocated for legislation. Although unions have generally not succeeded in getting legislation approved, they have been successful at negotiating the inclusion of VDT provisions in the contracts of some New York City employees[28] as well as some employees of the Social Security Administration.[29]

Still, neither the states nor the federal government have seriously attempted to utilize their authority, as acknowledged by the courts, to regulate workplace safety. Federal standards could be easily designed and implemented. Numerous other countries have been regulating VDT emissions and workstations for years, and computer manufacturers have complied.

International Standards

Electromagnetic emissions are measured in milligauss (mG). In 1986, Sweden's National Board for Measurement and Testing published a set of suggested voluntary guidelines for computer manufacturers, limiting emissions to 2.5 mG (at approximately two feet from the monitor).[30] Since then, these standards have become both mandatory and more stringent. Worldwide, Sweden's standards are considered exemplary in user safety.[31]

(Meanwhile, back in the United States, one computer expert measured emissions from his personal computer at 100 mG.)[32]

New Zealand also enacted impressive regulations in 1981. The Code of Practice[33] provides guidelines for the workplace that apply to manufacturers, suppliers of equipment, and employers. Standards for protection of the eyes, the musculoskeletal system, and the skin were established. Employers are also encouraged to allow pregnant VDT operators to transfer to non-VDT duties. Because the standards apply to new acquisitions but not existing equipment, businesses and corporations could comply with little added expense. Like Sweden, New Zealand is in the process of updating and tightening their standards.

On the whole, most European standards are more stringent than those in the United States. Computer manufacturers have responded to this demand by producing two models, one for European markets and one for American.

The Cost of Regulating

Ideally, regulations would provide for rest breaks, safe workstation equipment, limits on continuous usage, and, of course, the *option* of transferring to non-VDT work during pregnancy. Numerous other regulations could be implemented easily and inexpensively. Several simple modifications could greatly attenuate the effect of VDTs on pregnant women.

One common misconception is that most of the electromagnetic radiation emitted from VDTs comes from the screen. In fact, most of the radiation is emitted from the flyback transformer in the back of the computer monitor, followed by the sides and the top. Generally, the danger regarding exposure is not from the VDT operator's own computer monitor but rather from computers behind the operator. Many employers line computers up in rows, where the exhaust from the back of one VDT operator's monitor blows directly on the back of another operator. To protect employees from exposure, the back of computer monitors should face an area away from other employees, for example, toward a wall. Another feasible solution is to put greater distance between rows of operators, as electromagnetic radiation dissipates beyond a distance of three feet. These solutions are relatively inexpensive and if federally mandated, could greatly reduce the risks of exposure.

It would also be simple and inexpensive to require employers to periodically test the level of electromagnetic radiation emissions in the workplace. Regulations could specify acceptable emissions levels. Gauges are so inexpensive that they are currently marketed to the general public to allow private individuals to test emission levels in their own homes. Since employers insist that the current levels are safe anyway, periodic testing should pose no threat, and the expense would be limited to the one-time purchase of a gauge. It is quite inconsistent to protect employees from the hazard of breathing secondhand smoke but do nothing to monitor their exposure to electromagnetic radiation. Testing emissions could also protect an employer from unwarranted suits, since the record would show that emission levels were within the acceptable range.

Of course, the easiest solution would be to require that employees be fully informed on a number of issues. First and foremost, employees should know the risks that might be associated with VDT usage, so that they can make an informed decision. If they choose to take the risk of exposure to emissions, they should sign a release of liability. By not informing employees about potential risks, employers have in effect made the decision on the employees' behalf. This way of proceeding conflicts with both the Supreme Court's ruling in *Johnson Controls* and the Pregnancy Discrimination Act. In *Johnson Controls* the employer decided that women should not be exposed to lead because it posed too great a risk to them. In the case of VDTs, employers have decided that computer monitors do not pose a risk, so everyone can be safely exposed. It is not only the employees who may be harmed by such high-handedness; the employers are setting themselves up for liability suits.

Next, employees should be educated on how to effectively use the ergonomic equipment employers spend so much money on. Only a small percentage of employees know how to adjust their ergonomic workstation.[34] Sometimes these ergonomic workstations actually have an *adverse* effect on employee health when furniture is incorrectly adjusted. Since ergonomics may factor into the reproductive complications suffered by VDT operators, teaching employees how to adjust their workstations may alleviate the problem and at a low cost/high benefit ratio.

An alternative or complement to workplace regulation would be the regulation of computer manufacturers. VDT manufacturers in the United States already have the capability to turn out low-radiation models and VDT screens, or radiation shields (although the worth of these screens is debatable, since they filter emissions from the front of the monitor where emissions are the weakest). In addition, the demand for low-radiation models is beginning to increase in the United States as consumers have become more concerned with the potential health hazards associated with VDT usage. Computer manufacturers could be required to produce only low-emission models—the kind they already produce for the European market. This would not only make the workplace safer but reduce emissions in the overall environment as well. The automobile industry has been subject to comparable regulation for years.

If nothing else, manufacturers could be required to either put a warning label on the VDT itself or provide with the purchase of every VDT a pamphlet addressing safety issues (preferably both). The obvious benefit of a warning label is that every user of the VDT would be likely to see it, whereas not every user has equal access to packaging information when the VDT is in a work setting or public facility. Warning labels are routinely included on most products that represent a possible safety risk, from light fixtures to children's toys to dry cleaning bags. If worded correctly, they do not open the manufacturer up to liability but simply inform the consumer. For example, manufacturers of alcoholic beverages warn consumers of the potential hazard of drinking alcohol while pregnant but are not liable if a pregnant woman chooses to drink. Similarly, pamphlets could provide information without making the VDT manufacturer more vulnerable to liability. Since a link was suggested between cellular phones and brain cancer, cellular phone companies have been routinely including safety information with their instruction booklets. Currently, most people do not even realize that VDT usage has been associated with reproductive complications, and the few who have heard of the risks tend to believe that if they were serious, the government would have by now intervened with appropriate regulation. Many Americans operate under the assumption that the government is paternalistic and places the health and welfare of the common citizen over the interests of big business.

The Price of Not Regulating

In not supporting regulation, corporations are penny-wise but pound-foolish. Apparently the short-term expense is a deterrent. However, economical short-term solutions could diminish long-term expense. Conversely, a lack of intervention could result in lower productivity, higher health care costs, and employee disaffection. VDT-related injuries already afflict at least five million people in the United States,[35] costing corporations millions in health care claims, loss of productivity, and compensation premiums. And this is only the tip of the iceberg.

Lawsuits are cropping up, and it is only a matter of time before employers and manufacturers will routinely be sued for health problems attributable to VDT radiation. Litigants have already claimed that electromagnetic emissions from cellular phones, power lines, radar guns, and VDTs are linked to various health hazards, particularly cancer.[36] For instance, two airline reservations agents developed cervical cancer and died in 1980. In a lawsuit filed on their behalf, the plaintiffs argued that the cancers were caused by VDT exposure.[37] The court held for the manufacturer, in part because the plaintiffs did not present strong enough evidence for a relationship between VDTs and cervical cancer. However, a more compelling argument could be made today. The cost of litigation, especially if pursued to the appeals level, should provide employers with an incentive for regulation.

Product liability suits have also been filed regarding VDTs.[38] Product liability claims can be filed against anyone, from the manufacturer to the distributer to the employer, although the employer may be immune from liability in some cases under worker's compensation laws.[39] Product liability claims can focus on negligence (reasonable care was not exercised to protect consumers), or on strict liability (the product was defective or unreasonably dangerous). In the latter case, a manufacturer's failure to warn can become a pivotal issue. In any case, regulation could actually protect manufacturers and employers as well as employees. If emission standards were set, manufacturers and employers who met them could insulate themselves from liability. On the other hand, with no standards in place, manufacturers and employers regulate themselves and may become liable for unsafe conditions. *Johnson Controls* serves as a reminder of the hazards of self-regulation.

Manufacturers are beginning to realize the importance of protecting themselves and warding off liability. In 1992, Apple Computer, IBM Corporation, and Compaq Computer announced plans to contribute $2.25 million to create the VDT Health Research Foundation at Johns Hopkins University.[40] Although this sounds like, and may well be, a step in the right direction, it is important to note that the funding for this research comes from corporations with a vested interest in the outcome.

The Waiting Game

One influential politician has voiced concern over the VDT issue and advocated increased research and attention. In 1989, then-Senator Albert Gore underscored the need for more research on the relationship between VDTs and reproductive complications:

> There are still many unanswered questions about the potential health effects of VDTs and of electromagnetic fields generally, but there is no longer any doubt that this form of radiation can cause some biochemical changes. In my view that information alone is sufficient to warrant a renewed commitment on the part of government and private industry to study this issue and search for solutions to protect people.[41]

Obviously that renewed commitment has yet to be made.

It is estimated that over twenty million American women use VDTs in the workplace.[42] At this point the impact of VDTs on reproduction is unknown. Even if current models are harmless, the potential hazards of future VDTs are unknown. At worst, regulation would simply be a superfluous precaution. However, if VDTs really are dangerous, regulation could begin to control potential health hazards even before they emerge clearly and unambiguously. Instead legislators wait for research results. But without legislation researchers cannot find funding sources: businesses do not want to fund research that may result in potential liability issues for them, while government grants are often subject to political interference, as demonstrated by the NIOSH study.

The point of this chapter is not to convince the American public that VDTs cause miscarriages. The more critical concern is the way that the political agenda behind this issue has hindered research, so that now, more than fifteen years after clusters of miscarriages were first reported in possible association with VDT use, we still have no definitive findings and, most importantly, no constructive solutions or safeguards.

If there is a connection between VDTs and miscarriage, the individuals at greatest risk would probably be those women—for example, telephone operators, mail order clerks, and airline reservations clerks—who are exposed to massive emissions from numerous terminals lined up in small, poorly ventilated areas. The suboptimal working conditions combined with rigid work schedules make these jobs stressful. Ironically, many blue-collar parents of baby-boomers often labored under dangerous and physically debilitating conditions in the hopes of giving their children the superior education that would equip them to pursue safer occupations in healthier environments. However, only the types of hazards and physical stress have changed, not the levels.

It is curious that a health hazard that potentially affects a vast percentage of the population, mainly women, has been largely ignored. It appears that many politicians, and the government as a whole, are quick to regulate women's reproductive health and autonomy in such areas as abortion and substance abuse, even when it is clear that women do not benefit from the attempted surveillance. However, when regulation could enhance the health and welfare of women at the expense of corporate America, the government is extraordinarily slow to act. Even in the workplace, or perhaps especially in the workplace, reproductive issues are subject to political agendas. In the 1996 election, the politics of reproduction and the family once again played a pivotal role.

[5]

Politics and Reproductive Choice

∾

*E*ach state or federal election, every nomination to the Supreme Court, reminds Americans of the pivotal role that women's reproductive rights play in politics. In elections, some individuals vote solely on a candidate's stance regarding reproductive choice, that is, regarding abortion. Similarly, the selection and confirmation of Supreme Court justices has frequently turned on the nominee's interpretation of and opinions about *Roe v. Wade*. One appointment could disrupt the balance of the Supreme Court and affect the status of *Roe v. Wade* and the reproductive options of generations of women.

For most antichoice individuals, the "unborn" are human beings and have the same rights as all other citizens. Believing that there is no one to speak for the rights of the unborn, the pro-lifers attempt to speak for them. For prochoice individuals, the issue is often more equivocal. Consider the following example.

Mary and John have a newborn infant who was born with a serious liver defect. The baby will die if she does not receive a transplant within the next few days. Mary is not a compatible donor but John is. No other compatible donors are available. Doctors are sometimes able to transplant a portion of a liver, but there is no guarantee of success, and the operation also carries serious risks for the donor, including infection, hemorrhage, diminished liver capacity, and complications (sometimes fatal ones) from anesthesia. John is conflicted. He was never committed to having this baby in the first place. He perceives the risks to his own life to be significant, and he is philosophically opposed to surgery. Clearly John faces a tough choice, but it is *his* decision to make. Although it may be easy to determine what one believes John should do or what one would oneself do in the same situation, the question is, does anyone have the right to make this decision for John and force him to carry it out?

Prochoice advocates believe that, just as no one should be able to force John into a liver donation, so no one should be able to coerce a woman into bearing a child, since it is she who assumes the health risks and often the economic, social, and educational burdens. The woman should have bodily autonomy, the right to make her own decisions regarding her own body. This does not mean that all prochoice advocates are proabortion, or would choose to have abortions themselves. They simply believe that each woman should be able to make that choice *for herself.* Since no one can definitively establish when life begins, it is up to each woman to determine whether her fetus represents a human life or not and whether she can bear the responsibility for the decision that she makes.

Abortion in the United States

It is no coincidence that when contraceptive research, education, and availability declines, reliance on abortion increases. For example, in the 1960s and 1970s over twenty pharmaceutical companies conducted research on birth control. Public funding for contraceptive services significantly declined in the 1980s,[1] and in 1996 only one company is doing research on birth control. Correspondingly, the number of legal abortions in the United States rose from 744,600 in 1973 (the year *Roe v. Wade* was decided) to 1,034,200 in 1975 to 1,588,600 in 1985.[2] This represents approximately one-fourth of all pregnancies in the United States. It is estimated that 46 percent of all American women will have an abortion by the age of forty-five.[3]

Birth control and abortion techniques have existed for centuries. Birth control methods have included ingesting such unappealing concoctions as "contraceptive fudge," which contained quinine, borax, salicylic acid, and cocoa butter, or using woolen tampons. Hippocrates reportedly invented an early version of the intrauterine device (IUD), consisting of a hollow lead tube that was filled with fat and inserted into the uterus. He apparently also advised patients on how to interrupt a pregnancy.[4]

In the early years of the American republic, common law determined the legal status of contraception and abortion. Under the common law, termination of a pregnancy before "quickening," the first apparent fetal movement, was permitted. Abortion was widely practiced and less likely to be perceived as morally wrong than it is today. However, in the 1800s, laws against birth control and abortion were enacted, culminating in the Comstock Act of 1873, a federal statute that massively restricted access to information about contraception and abortion. These laws were at least partially influenced by lobbying from the medical profession. Lobbying led to licensing laws that eliminated many potential providers of abortion services, such as midwives, and gave the medical profession control over abortion and other obstetric/gynecological procedures. Ironically, one hundred years later, the American Medical Association (AMA) came forward as one of the strongest advocates of safe, legal abortions, after viewing firsthand the consequences of illegal ones.

Some scholars believe that the Comstock Act was the all-male legislature's attempt to subdue the developing independence of women and inhibit changes in the family structure, including declining size.[5] In any case, exactly one hundred years before *Roe v. Wade,* the United States first statutorily restricted access to contraception and abortion.

Many people are amazed to learn that married couples were not guaranteed the right to be free from criminal prosecution for using contraceptives *until 1965.* Prior to that date, some states had laws against either using contraceptives or aiding and abetting another individual in the use of them.[6] In Connecticut, for example, it was a crime, punishable by a fine, imprisonment, or both, for anyone to attempt to prevent conception. Another Connecticut statute made it possible to apply similar penalties to anyone who assisted in contraceptive use. When the director of a Planned Parenthood clinic and a physician were arrested for violating these statutes, they challenged their constitutionality. The United States Supreme Court ruled that such laws violated an individual's constitutional rights unless the state could demonstrate that a compelling state interest was at stake.

Two aspects of this decision were extremely innovative. The first was the application of the "strict scrutiny" criterion to state laws on contraception. In deciding whether a state law is constitutional, the Supreme Court can use one of two approaches or standards. If the "rational basis" standard is adopted, the state only needs to demonstrate that there is a rational basis or legitimate purpose for the law that is reasonably related to some permissible governmental interest, and the law will not be found to violate the individual's constitutional rights. This is fairly easy to accomplish, and laws are generally upheld when the Supreme Court uses this approach. With the "strict scrutiny" approach, on the other hand, the state must demonstrate that it has a "compelling interest" in the issue or the law will be found unconstitutional because it violates an individual's constitutional rights. It is much more difficult for a state to demonstrate a compelling interest, so this standard is the more rigorous of the two tests. In 1965, the majority of the members of the Supreme Court chose to use the strict-scrutiny standard for this contraception statute.

The other innovative aspect of this decision was the Supreme Court's finding that contraception laws violated an individual's right to privacy. The Constitution does not explicitly cite a fundamental right to privacy, but the court deduced it from the Bill of Rights, particularly the First, Third, Fourth, Fifth, and Ninth Amendments. These amendments assure that citizens will enjoy freedom of speech and assembly; that they cannot be required to house soldiers except in time of war; that they will be protected from unreasonable searches and seizures; and that they will not be deprived of life, liberty, or property without due process of law. Furthermore, the Fourteenth Amendment requires the states to uphold most of the provisions of the Bill of Rights. Therefore, no state could enact a law that would violate these provisions, or the newly derived right to privacy.

Once the Supreme Court had "fashioned" the right to privacy, several quick decisions expanded this right. In 1972 the Court found in *Eisenstadt v. Baird* that the right to privacy in contraceptive decisions extended to unmarried couples.[7] Then, in 1973, Norma McCorvey (better known by the pseudonym Roe), a woman who could not afford to travel to a state where abortion was legal and safe, became the primary plaintiff in a class action suit challenging a Texas statute that criminalized abortion except to save the life of the mother. The case became one of the most controversial in the history of the Supreme Court. In *Roe v. Wade* the Supreme Court applied the strict-scrutiny test and held that the Texas statute violated McCorvey's right to privacy.

In fashioning its opinion, the Court attempted to balance the woman's right to privacy, the rights of the state, and the rights of the fetus. The Court ruled that the state has a compelling interest in the potential life the fetus represents but not until after the point of viability, the point at which the fetus can survive on its own outside the uterus. In short, the unborn were not elevated to personhood. "State regulation protective of fetal life after viability thus has both logical and biological justifications. If the state is interested in protecting fetal life after viability, it may go so far as to proscribe abortion during that period, except when it is necessary to preserve the life or health of the mother."[8] At that time, a fetus was not generally considered viable before the third trimester of the pregnancy. Medical technology has now extended the range of viability to the latter part of the second trimester.

In short, prior to viability, the state's interest in the fetus was not deemed compelling enough to override the woman's right to privacy.

> The detriment that the state would impose upon the pregnant woman by denying the choice altogether is apparent. Specific and direct harm medically diagnosable even in early pregnancy may be involved. Maternity, or additional offspring, may force upon the woman a distressful life and future. Psychological harm may be imminent. Mental and physical health may be taxed by child care. There is also the distress, for all concerned, associated with the unwanted child, and there is the problem of bringing a child

into a family, already unable, psychologically and otherwise, to care for it. In other cases, as in this one, the additional difficulties and continuing stigma of unwed motherhood may be involved. All these are factors the woman and her responsible physician necessarily will consider in consultation.[9]

The Court ruled that the state also had a compelling interest in the life and health of the mother. However, since the mortality rate for childbirth is greater than that for first-trimester abortion, the Court found that the states could not demonstrate a compelling interest for prohibiting abortion in the first trimester in order to preserve and protect maternal health.

Since 1973 the constitutionality of numerous state laws restricting abortion access has been challenged before the Supreme Court. This has placed the status of *Roe v. Wade* in jeopardy. Although *Roe v. Wade* still stands as good law, some of the decisions have whittled away at the fundamental right to privacy in abortion decisions. It is interesting to note that over one-third of such challenges have originated in two states, Missouri and Pennsylvania.[10] Although the challenges have remained similar over the last two decades, the Supreme Court decisions have shifted. This was seen most dramatically in 1989, when the impact of several conservative justices, appointed during the Reagan administration, began to be felt. These appointments altered the temper of the Court and its positions on several issues.

One issue that has come up several times is the requirement of informed consent. Informing patients of treatment options and of the possible risks associated with each one is good medical practice. However, the informed-consent statutes that have been challenged include provisions that go beyond this, such as a requirement that women seeking an abortion receive information on fetal development or wait for twenty-four hours before undergoing the procedure. Initially the Court found these provisions unconstitutional.[11] Nevertheless, in 1992, the Supreme Court ruled that a Pennsylvania law requiring a woman to sign an informed and then wait twenty-four hours before receiving an abortion was constitutional.[12] This waiting period is no minor problem for women who live in rural areas and have to travel hours to reach providers. Abortion is not available in 83 percent of all counties in the United States, and in South Dakota there is only one abortion provider in the entire state.[13] Moreover, given the increasing violence of the antichoice contingent, requiring a woman to visit an abortion-providing facility more than once may be putting her in considerable peril.

The Supreme Court's rulings regarding parental consent/notification statutes have also been contradictory. Many states have enacted laws requiring women under the age of eighteen to either notify or obtain the permission of one parent before undergoing an abortion. Initially, the Court found that requiring parental consent or notification violated the minor's right to privacy.[14] In *Planned Parenthood v. Danforth*, the Court wrote

> Just as with the requirement of consent from the spouse, so here, the State does not have the constitutional authority to give a third party an absolute, and possibly arbitrary, veto over the decision of the physician and his patient to terminate the patient's pregnancy, regardless of the reason for withholding the consent. . . . Constitutional rights do not mature and come into being magically only when one attains the state-defined age of majority.[15]

However, in more recent challenges to parental consent statutes, the Supreme Court has found them to be constitutional, particularly if the woman has access to a judicial bypass.[16] A judicial bypass is a means by which a minor can petition the court to waive the parental-consent requirement. The judge may or may not agree to this, and obtaining the bypass can take

weeks. Often by the time a minor has determined and acknowledged that she is pregnant, she may be quite advanced in her
pregnancy. She may not have time to attempt a judicial bypass
if she hopes to have the abortion during the first trimester, the
time when the procedure is safest and least traumatic. In addition, the intimidation of the judicial system may dissuade many
young women from even attempting a judicial bypass.

One young woman, Becky Bell, the subject of a recent docu-
mentary,[17] found the judicial bypass an insurmountable obstacle. When Becky learned she was pregnant, she confronted the
father of the child. He wanted no responsibility in the matter.
Too embarrassed to tell one of her parents and obtain consent,
and convinced that a judicial bypass was unlikely, she sought an
illegal abortion. Becky became one of many young women who
die each year from the medical complications of an illegal abortion. Even if there is a judicial-bypass option, the Court has held
that a statute requiring notification/consent of *both* parents is
unconstitutional.[18]

The Supreme Court has also rendered mixed opinions on the
constitutionality of statutes that require a physician to perform
viability tests on women seeking abortions during the second
trimester. Initially, the Court found such statutes vague.[19] But
eventually a statute that denied women past the point of viability access to abortion was upheld.[20]

The Court's rulings have, however, been consistent on other
issues. For example, laws that require women to notify their
husbands and/or obtain their consent prior to obtaining an
abortion have been struck down by the Supreme Court as unconstitutional.[21] Similarly, the Supreme Court has consistently
struck down statutes requiring that second-trimester abortions
be performed in hospitals,[22] although it has allowed a statute
requiring that second-trimester abortions be performed in licensed clinics.[23]

Supreme Court rulings on the use of federal funds for abortions have also been consistent. Overall, the Court has repeatedly held that statutes limiting or denying the use of federal funds for abortions are constitutional,[24] even though federal funds can be and are used for pregnancy and childbirth procedures (and even for sterilizations). In other words, a woman receiving Medicaid can use that coverage to pay for her prenatal care and delivery but not for an abortion. This can create a serious obstacle to abortion for women of low income. The Court has also held that publically funded hospitals are not required to perform abortions[25] and that statutes prohibiting the use of federally funded employees or facilities in abortion procedures are constitutional.[26] In fact, President Reagan implemented an administrative provision which made it impossible for employees of clinics receiving federal funds to even discuss the option of abortion with pregnant women without jeopardizing their federal funding. This infamous "gag rule" was found constitutional by the Supreme Court[27] but was voided by executive order two days after President Clinton took office.

The Supreme Court has also dodged some potentially controversial issues. When the Missouri legislature approved a preamble to a statute that stated "life begins at conception," the Court deferred ruling on the constitutionality of the preamble since it did not regulate abortion per se but simply expressed a value judgment of the state.[28]

One of the most recent cases to be heard before the Supreme Court bears noting. In *Bray v. Alexandria Women's Health Clinic*,[29] the prochoice plaintiffs attempted to use a statute from the 1800s, originally aimed at the Ku Klux Klan, to prevent antiabortion protesters from blockading clinics. The Supreme Court held that such an application was unconstitutional. (Later Congress enacted a law protecting access to clinics.) In another case, prochoice advocates successfully brought an action against a coalition of antichoice groups, alleging that they were involved in a nationwide conspiracy to close abortion clinics and were thus in violation of RICO (Racketeer Influenced and Corrupt Organizations Act).[30] This issue will probably come before the Supreme Court again, as violence toward clinics increases.

The success or failure of these challenges is largely due to the composition of the Supreme Court. Presidents Reagan and Bush, who openly voiced their antichoice convictions, were able to appoint a number of justices to the Supreme Court who shared their views. For example, Clarence Thomas, who maintained during Senate confirmation hearings that he had no opinion on *Roe v. Wade,* has repeatedly revealed his antichoice stance since his appointment to the Supreme Court. Other judges, such as Chief Justice Rehnquist and Justice Scalia, object to the use of the strict-scrutiny test to evaluate abortion statutes and believe that the rational-basis test would be more appropriate. If more justices are appointed who agree with Rehnquist and Scalia, it is likely that *Roe v. Wade* will be overturned, given the ease with which the rational-basis requirement can be satisfied.

Justice Sandra Day O'Connor has fashioned her own test, which some refer to as a middle-ground approach. O'Connor applies the strict-scrutiny test only when the law in question creates an *undue burden* on a woman's right to abortion. An undue burden is a substantial obstacle imposed by the state to limit access. Otherwise, O'Connor uses the rational-basis test. Justices Kennedy and Souter have also come to share her approach. Thus the majority of justices currently on the Supreme Court either do not apply the strict-scrutiny test to abortion statutes or apply it only in selected instances.

The justices who vigorously defended a woman's right to choose, such as Thurgood Marshall, William Brennan, and Harry Blackmun (the author of the *Roe v. Wade* decision), have all retired. Of the nine justices currently on the Supreme Court, three—Rehnquist, Scalia, and Thomas—have repeatedly voted against the test set forth in *Roe v. Wade*. Justice White (who originally opposed *Roe v. Wade* in 1973) was recently replaced by Justice Ginsberg, but it is not yet clear how Ginsberg or Justice Breyer, who recently replaced Blackmun, will vote on abortion issues.

In the meantime, Norma McCorvey, the woman who allowed herself to be named as plaintiff in *Roe v. Wade,* underwent her own conversion. In August 1995, McCorvey was baptized by the national director of the antichoice group Operation Rescue and announced that she no longer supported a woman's right to choose abortion *after the first trimester.* When Sarah Weddington, one of the attorneys who argued *Roe v. Wade* for the plaintiffs before the Supreme Court, learned of McCorvey's attitude change she stated, "I'm shocked. At a time when we are working so hard to campaign for people who are pro-choice and not having much luck, I didn't need this one." [31]

A Possible Scenario

If *Roe v. Wade* were overturned, each state would then be able to frame its own policy on abortion. Many states would probably revert back to the statutes they had on their books prior to the 1973 decision. Conservative states would likely make abortion illegal or strictly limit access, while more liberal states would likely permit it in a relatively broad range of circumstances. Therefore, women with access to money who wanted to terminate a pregnancy but who lived in a state where abortion was illegal could travel to an abortion-friendly state, but a poor woman in the same situation would be confronted with several decisions.

She could have and keep the child, possibly worsening her

economic plight. She could give the child up for adoption. Note, however, that there are presently over a million children waiting to be adopted in the United States alone. Contrary to the picture painted by the popular media, we suffer from an extreme shortage of adoptive *parents,* not *children,* a crisis that prompted Speaker of the House Newt Gingrich to suggest the revival of the orphanage. Although there can be a *short* waiting period (less than two years) for healthy white infants, there is very little demand for other children and therefore virtually no delay in adopting. This does not include the enormous numbers of infants and children who are literally starving to death and are available for adoption through international agencies.

Women could also decide to pursue an illegal, unsafe abortion. Historical data suggests that when a woman desperately wants to terminate a pregnancy, she will do so even at the risk of her life. Prior to *Roe v. Wade* approximately 10,000 women died every year in the United States from illegal abortions. Today, worldwide, approximately 200,000 women die each year from botched abortions. If *Roe v. Wade* were overturned, hazardous, illegal abortions would again become one way out of an unwanted pregnancy for thousands of women, especially those of low income.

If the fetus were to be acknowledged by the Court as a person, with constitutionally protected rights, certain postcoital contraceptives, such as intrauterine devices (IUDs) and so-called "morning after" pills, could be banned. Postcoital contraceptives are contragestives, meaning that they prevent, not the fertilization of the egg, but the implantation of the embryo. For example, the IUD irritates the endometrium and makes it inhospitable to implantation, so that even if the embryo does manage to attach itself, it will probably be spontaneously aborted. If life is deemed to begin at fertilization, such devices could become illegal.

IVF practices could also be affected. Frozen embryos could have all the legal protection afforded to persons, and the law might require implantation. Other laws could restrict the number of embryos implanted because selective abortion, to terminate multiple pregnancies that threaten the life or health of the embryos or the mother, might run into legal obstacles. Even the use of fertility drugs could be drastically affected.[32]

The "Abortion Pill"

The struggle to obtain Food and Drug Administration (FDA) approval for one drug, a virtual icon of reproductive freedom and choice, embodies the entire conflict. Although RU-486[33] has been termed the "abortion pill," it can be used as a precoital contraceptive, a postcoital contraceptive, or an abortifacient (an agent that induces abortion). Some researchers have even suggested that RU-486 may eventually be available as a male contraceptive.[34] In addition, it may prove to be an effective treatment for a variety of illnesses, some of them terminal.

Each new menstrual cycle, an ovum begins to mature within the ovary. The ovum is surrounded by a follicle which is composed of tissue. When ovulation occurs, the ripe ovum then erupts from the follicle into the woman's abdominal cavity and is usually pulled into the fallopian tube. The follicle, now termed the corpus luteum, begins to secrete progesterone, which promotes the thickening of the endometrium (the lining of the uterus) in preparation for possible implantation. If implantation occurs, the progesterone sustains the embryo until the formation of the placenta. If implantation does not occur, the corpus luteum will gradually degenerate, and the decline in progesterone (and other hormones) will trigger the onset of the next menstrual cycle.

RU-486, or mifepristone, is a chemical compound that acts as a progesterone inhibiter. It prevents progesterone from entering the cells of the endometrium. The endometrium therefore does not thicken in response to ovulation, and the onset of the next menstrual cycle is triggered. Since progesterone is an essential component in any pregnancy and has a pervasive effect on the menstrual cycle, RU-486 can be used as a contraceptive in two ways. First, low doses can be administered throughout the menstrual cycle or in the latter half of it. RU-486 is thus comparable to the standard birth control pill, but does not expose the user to multiple hormones and can be taken on a more flexible schedule. For example, a woman only needs to use RU-486 during months when she is sexually active and can discontinue use at other times. Currently, in the countries where RU-486 is available, it is not frequently used as a contraceptive.

RU-486 can also be used as a postcoital contraceptive, when a chosen method of birth control fails (e.g., when a condom breaks or when contraceptives were not used). IUDs are another example of postcoital contraceptives, but can cause discomfort, increase the risk of pelvic inflammatory disease, and occasionally perforate the uterus.

The "Morning After" Pill

Sexually assaulted women are often offered a postcoital contraceptive commonly called the "morning after" pill. Like RU-486 the "morning after" pill uses hormonal manipulation to induce a menstrual cycle. Some forms of the "morning after" pill contain DES (see note 24, chapter 2). The most common form, Ovral, is not a singular pill but rather a regimen combining several of the synthetic estrogen/progesterone pills.[35] The first dosage of the "morning after" pill must be taken within seventy-two hours after intercourse, followed by a second dosage twelve hours later. The postcoital effectiveness rates for the "morning after" pill and RU-486 are similar, although the rate for RU-486 is slightly higher.[36] However, women seem to experience more physical side effects from the "morning after" pill, such as nausea and vomiting. On the other hand, they report a greater delay in the onset of their next menstrual cycle from RU-486.[37]

Recent survey results indicate that 133 out of 170 Planned Parenthood clinics and 20 out of 22 university clinics will prescribe the "morning after" pill if a woman requests it within seventy-two hours of unprotected intercourse.[38] Most of these clinics, particularly those in university settings, have had a "morning after" pill available for over twenty years. Still, on the whole, neither physicians nor the general public know much about the "morning after" pill. This lack of awareness may be due in part to the absence of FDA approval for a "morning after" pill, although the drugs have been approved for other purposes (e.g., birth control). Once a drug is approved by the FDA, it is possible for physicians to prescribe it for nonapproved purposes.

Wyeth-Ayerst, the pharmaceutical company that manufactures Ovral, has no incentive to seek FDA approval for its use as a postcoital contraceptive. First, the expense involved in demonstrating its safety and efficacy for this purpose would not be balanced by any comparable gain in sales, since the drug would not be consistently prescribed to any patient. Second, approval of Ovral as a postcoital contraceptive would open the company up to liability suits and boycotts. As it stands, if a physician prescribes it for nonapproved uses, he or she bears most of the liability, unless an inherent defect in the drug is discovered. However, the lack of FDA approval makes the drug unavailable as a postcoital contraceptive to a tremendous number of women if their physicians are unaware of alternative uses.

Moreover, federally funded clinics cannot dispense a drug for nonapproved purposes unless federal funds (Title X) are not used in the process. There are relatively few clinics that do *not* use federal funds. The other postcoital contraceptive, RU-486, has not been approved by the FDA because of its abortifacient properties.

RU-486 as an Abortifacient

Many people believe that RU-486, should the FDA approve it, will make abortion as simple as getting a prescription filled at a pharmacy. Purportedly women will now be able to terminate pregnancies in the privacy of their own homes. As a consequence, it is feared that attitudes toward abortion will become nonchalant. This misconception springs from ignorance of how RU-486 works as an abortifacient.

RU-486 is administered orally within the first few weeks of pregnancy. The earlier it is taken, the more effective it is.[39] The entire process requires three or four visits with a physician. During the first visit, an ultrasound is often conducted to determine the woman's gestational stage and if she is a suitable candidate (with regard to her health) for treatment. The drug may or may not be administered during the first visit. In France, there is a one-week waiting period between the first visit and administration of the drug. The drug's antiprogesterone properties cause the endometrium to deteriorate, which in turn causes the natural secretion of prostaglandins, the hormones that assist in the expulsion of menstrual tissue by inducing contractions in the uterus.

Typically, about two days after the administration of RU-486, the woman typically returns to the physician to receive synthetic prostaglandins as well. Originally, synthetic prostaglandins were administered through injections, but now they are generally administered orally. Oral administration reduces the rate of absorption, which seems to enhance the safety, convenience, and effectiveness of the product.[40] Misoprostol (or Cytotec), a drug commonly used to treat stomach ulcers, now substitutes for synthetic prostaglandin injections—much to the chagrin of Cytotec's manufacturer, the Searle Corporation (a subsidiary of Monsanto), for antiabortionists have threatened it with product boycotts even though Searle does not market the drug as an abortifacient. In fact, the product information flier that accompanies prescriptions of Cytotec clearly warns against the use of the drug during pregnancy.

The embryo is usually expelled several hours after administration of the prostaglandin, often while the woman waits in the physician's office. However, she must return in approximately two weeks to determine if the process has been successful. If used early in the pregnancy and taken in combination with synthetic prostaglandins, RU-486 is approximately 95 to 99 percent effective.[41] In France, if the treatment does not work, the woman must agree to have a surgical abortion, since the drugs may have damaged the fetus.

Most *known* side effects from RU-486 are relatively short-lived, usually ceasing within forty-eight hours after administration. These include nausea, vomiting, diarrhea, breast tenderness, headache, fatigue, and abdominal cramps. Some abdominal cramping is painful enough to require analgesics. Severe uterine bleeding can last over a week, with about one in five hundred women requiring blood transfusions. A few women (six in five hundred) experience a significant drop in blood pressure. Some of these side effects are directly attributable to RU-486, but most result from the combination of RU-486 with synthetic prostaglandins. The long-term effects of RU-486, particularly on future fertility and the immune system, are not yet known.

Of the more than 150,000 women who have used RU-486, three suffered heart attacks, one of which was fatal. Each of these women reportedly had other "risk factors" that may have led to the complications (the woman who died was a heavy smoker and was undergoing her thirteenth abortion.) As a result, the drug is not recommended for women who smoke or who have or have had fibroids, circulation problems, high blood pressure, diabetes, severe bronchitis, glaucoma, ulcers, colitis, anemia, blood clotting problems, adrenal gland problems, heart disease, high cholesterol, a recent caesarean section, asthma, heart problems, pelvic inflammatory disease, or abnormal menstrual cycles. It is also not recommended for women over thirty-five years old or those more than seven weeks pregnant. In addition, only specially trained physicians should administer the drug and only when cardiovascular monitoring equipment, resuscitation medication/equipment, and emergency facilities are available.

Contrast abortions brought on by RU-486 with the typical surgical abortion. If the pregnancy is in its first trimester, generally a procedure known as a D & E (dilation and evacuation) or vacuum aspiration is performed: the cervix is dilated, and the contents of the uterus are removed through suctioning. If the abortion is performed early in the pregnancy, the woman may not need an anesthetic at all or only a local one.

Occasionally, if some products of pregnancy remain, the woman may have to undergo a D & C (dilation and curettage). The cervix is dilated and the walls of the uterus scraped. The D & C used to be the standard procedure for abortion, but it has many more risks than a D & E, including the use of a general anesthetic, and is less frequently used today.

There can be many side effects from a surgical abortion, including hemorrhaging, abdominal pain and cramping, and nausea. If the pregnancy has advanced beyond sixteen weeks, saline or synthetic prostaglandin is often injected into the amniotic sac to induce labor. Labor compounds the risk from the abortion. The overall risk of death from a legal, surgical abortion in the United States was estimated in 1985 to be 0.4 per 100,000.

For women in the United States, RU-486 would not necessarily be an easier or cheaper way to terminate a pregnancy and is slightly *less* successful than surgical abortion. RU-486 may require more visits and take more overall time than most surgical abortions. Unless a twenty-four-hour waiting period is imposed after the signing of the informed consent, surgical abortion generally requires two visits, one for the actual procedure and one for a follow-up exam. Given the greater number of appointments needed when RU-486 is the abortifacient of choice, it may prove even more costly than surgery.

However, RU-486 is probably safer. It is also less invasive: women report feeling more in control of the process and their bodies. Additionally, RU-486 can be administered earlier in the pregnancy, and unless the procedure is unsuccessful, surgery, with its risks of infection, injury, and anesthesia complications, is eliminated. Some women report that the psychological toll is greater with RU-486; some report that it is greater with surgical abortions.

Why RU-486 Isn't Available in the United States

RU-486 was synthesized in 1980 by a French researcher named Etienne-Emile Baulieu and was later developed by the drug company Roussel-Uclaf (hence the initials *RU*). In 1988, the

French government approved the use of RU-486 as an abortifacient, but Roussel-Uclaf withdrew it from the French market in response to protests from the Catholic Church and threatened boycotts. Additionally, some of the wives and children of Roussel-Uclaf executives were receiving anonymous threats.[42] Moreover, 55 percent of Roussel-Uclaf is owned by Hoechst A. G., whose chief executive officer is a devout Catholic.

Eventually, the French minister of health overruled Roussel-Uclaf's withdrawal, calling RU-486 the "moral property of women." Cynics suggested that this action was motivated by the French government's financial interest in the drug (it owns 35 percent of Roussel-Uclaf) or was an effort to absolve Roussel-Uclaf of moral responsibility in the public's eye and thus allow it to reap its profits. The company denied the latter allegation.[43]

Similar protests were staged in the United States, even though the antichoice administrations of Reagan and Bush neither invited nor supported the marketing of RU-486. In fact, the FDA specifically banned the importation of RU-486. Under the Federal Food, Drug and Cosmetic Act of 1938,[44] before any drug can be introduced into interstate commerce it must be found safe. In 1962 that act was expanded to ensure that drugs introduced into interstate commerce were not only safe but also effective. To obtain FDA approval, a new drug must first be sponsored by a drug manufacturer, who submits an Investigational New Drug application.[45] Next, the safety and effectiveness of the drug must be supported by research findings, which are submitted, along with information about the drug and its possible uses, to the FDA. Technically, the FDA must reject or accept the application within 180 days, but extensions are common.

In July 1988 the FDA introduced a new program, called Pilot Guidance, which allowed unapproved drugs that posed no safety risk to be imported in small quantities by individuals for personal use. Forty drugs were excluded from importation. RU-486 was not excluded, however, it was quickly added to the exclusion list in response to political pressure from congressmen.

The validity of this exclusion was tested in July 1992, when Abortion Rights Mobilization, a prochoice group, flew Leona Benten, who reportedly feared a surgical abortion, to England to obtain RU-486 to terminate her pregnancy. When Benten attempted to bring the drug back with her to the United States, it was confiscated by U.S. Customs at Kennedy Airport in New York City. Benten sued the FDA, alleging that it acted illegally in confiscating the drug. While the district court ruled in Benten's favor, the appeals court blocked the district court's decision and the U.S. Supreme Court upheld the ban. Benten subsequently had a surgical abortion.

In effect the ban quashed all research on RU-486. In part this was due to the ban itself and in part to the hostile environment it created. Although an exception to the importation ban might have been made for research purposes, few people were willing to conduct or fund research on a drug so controversial. Moreover, Roussel-Uclaf, which held the patent rights, would not sponsor the drug for FDA approval while powerful sectors of the American public were so hostile to it. The company decided that, in order for them to export the drug as an abortifacient,

the importing country would have to satisfy five conditions: (1) Abortion must be legal. (2) It must be widely accepted by "public opinion." (3) A suitable prostaglandin must be available. (4) Distribution must be under tight official control, as with narcotics. (5) Patients must sign a letter agreeing to a surgical abortion if the pill failed. In practice, there was a sixth condition: the company would not sanction exports unless ranking government officials urged them to do so.[46]

Although the United States could have seized the patent rights from Roussel-Uclaf if the public interest was at stake, neither the Reagan nor the Bush administration interpreted the unavailability of RU-486 as a threat to the public interest. At this point the possibility of RU-486 becoming available to American consumers seemed remote. In fact, Congressman Ron Wyden referred to the ban and the withholding of FDA approval as "medical McCarthyism."

Then, in 1992, the political climate for RU-486 began to change, with the election of Bill Clinton as president. On 22 January 1993, Clinton's third day in office, he signed a presidential memorandum encouraging the Department of Health and Human Services to facilitate testing and licensing of RU-486 in the United States. In his memorandum, Clinton suggested that the FDA ban may have been prompted by considerations other than the safety of the drug. Next, in April 1993, the American Medical Association (AMA), which had supported legalizing RU-486 since 1990, and the American College of Obstetricians and Gynecologists (ACOG) urged Roussel-Uclaf to apply for FDA approval so that the drug could be made available in the United States. Finally, even the FDA became more hospitable: it indicated that further clinical trials might not even be necessary in order to gain approval.[17] Roussel-Uclaf could no longer claim that there was an environment hostile to RU-486 in the United States.

After a year of negotiations (and prodding from the Clinton administration), in May 1994 Roussel-Uclaf agreed to relinquish the technology and patent rights for RU-486 to the Population Council, a nonprofit contraception research group.[48] Roussel-Uclaf received no remuneration in exchange but did secure immunity from liability. This factor weighed heavily with the company, given the liability issues related to birth control devices. (Roussel-Uclaf probably did not perceive that the market value of RU-486 would offset the liability.) Roussel-Uclaf also received some insulation from boycotts. However, shortly after the agreement was reached, antichoice contingencies targeted several Roussel-Uclaf and Hoechst products for boycott, attempting to "persuade" them to rescind the license agreement. The Population Council immediately assured the general public that Roussel-Uclaf no longer had legal rights to the patent, and the boycott waned.

As of 1996, the import ban on RU-486 remains in effect, but the Population Council is attempting to begin research trials on its use as an abortifacient. The research is scheduled to include two thousand women enrolled in ten to twelve different clinics across the United States. Eventually, the Population Council will probably seek FDA approval for the drug and an American manufacturer and distributor. (Reportedly dozens of manufacturers, most with limited product lines, have declared themselves willing to act as distributors.)

In 1994, the World Health Organization (WHO) launched an investigation into the use of RU-486 as a postcoital contraceptive. The only American research site scheduled was San Francisco General Hospital. In May 1994, within twenty-four hours of the first advertisements, eighty women in that city volunteered to participate in the study. In San Francisco alone, twenty-one hundred women were administered the drug to assist in determining the optimal dose for preventing pregnancy. In two previous studies, RU-486 was found to be 100 percent effective as a postcoital contraceptive. If the drug is approved as a postcoital contraceptive, it can also be used, though not marketed, as an abortifacient. However, regardless of the results, it is unlikely that WHO, which would oversee the distribution of RU-486 to nonindustrialized countries, would act in opposition to American sentiment, because WHO receives significant financial backing from the United States.

Supporters of RU-486 would like to see the approval process expedited, in case future presidential elections result in an antichoice administration. If and when it is approved it will probably be for very limited purposes.

Antichoice forces are not alone in their opposition to RU-486. Some prochoice feminists also oppose approval, although for very different reasons. Politics makes strange bedfellows.

Opposition to RU-486

In contrast to the very vocal and very visible antichoice contingencies, most people in the United States would like to keep abortions legal and most believe that RU-486 should be made available to the American public. On the abortion issue, the Clinton administration appears to represent the views of the majority.

To antiabortionists, RU-486 is a "human pesticide," destroying "life," as they define it. This is inarguable, since it represents a personal, often religious, belief. A second concern is that RU-486 will make abortion easier, hence more common, and that attitudes toward abortion will become more casual. The available data do not support these notions. Since RU-486 was introduced in France in 1988, the abortion rate has not increased. In fact, one could argue that RU-486 actually lowers the abortion rate: when used as a postcoital contraceptive, it makes the uterus unfavorable to pregnancy, but technically an abortion is not performed. This however provides little solace for those who believe life begins at conception.

Prolifers also maintain that they are concerned over health risks to women. This is also the main concern for some prochoice feminists. For example, Janice Raymond[49] argues that RU-486 is dangerous and that its long-term effects are unknown. She refers to the drug as a "chemical brew" or "drug cocktail." This is a valid concern. However, the lack of widespread, independent research on the safety of RU-486 is not atypical, especially within the area of women's reproductive health. Historically, many obstetric/gynecological procedures were used without being thoroughly investigated. Additionally, many obstetric/gynecological medications prescribed for women were not adequately researched. Moreover, *many* current procedures and prescriptions lack empirical support, and a number of these threaten women's general health, their reproductive health, or their lives. Clearly, there is no need to add to the list.

Notwithstanding, for a pharmaceutical, RU-486 has amassed a tremendous amount of supportive data. Since 1988, 150,000 to 200,000 women have taken the drug. Other postcoital contraceptives and abortifacients currently in use have less or no research support. For example, it is impossible to know the long-term effects of birth control pills until the first generation of women who used them for prolonged periods become menopausal and/or postmenopausal. There is scant research on the effects of using Ovral as a postcoital contraceptive, yet thousands of women are prescribed the drug each year. A drug containing DES is still prescribed as an emergency postcoital contraceptive. On the face of it, at least, RU-486 seems safer than any of these drugs, since it blocks the production of natural hormones rather than introducing synthetic ones into the body.

Perhaps more importantly, at this point the concept of a chemical postcoital contraceptive/abortifacient is so well known (and accepted) that, if RU-486 is not made available in the United States, physicians and agencies who have concocted alternatives—true "chemical brews"—may put women's health at a greater risk. In August 1995, the prestigious *New England Journal of Medicine* published a study by Richard U. Hausknecht, a New York gynecologist, who combined two readily available prescription drugs, misoprostol (Cytotec) and methotrexate, to induce abortion. Cytotec is the synthetic prostaglandin commonly used with RU-486. Methotrexate is a treatment used for arthritis, cancer, and asthma. Excerpts from one popular guide to prescription drugs include the following cautions regarding methotrexate.

> Methotrexate can be extremely toxic, even in the relatively low doses prescribed for rheumatoid arthritis. This drug should be considered "last-resort" therapy for non-cancer therapies to be used only for severe cases that have not responded to other treatments. Methotrexate should be prescribed only by doctors who are familiar with the drug and its potential for producing toxic effects. . . . Methotrexate can trigger a unique and dangerous form of lung disease at any time during the course of therapy. . . . Methotrexate can cause severe reduction in red- and white-blood-cell and blood platelet counts. . . . Methotrexate can cause severe diarrhea, stomach irritation, and mouth or gum sores. Death can result from intestinal perforation caused by methotrexate. . . . The most common side effects are liver irritation, loss of kidney function, reduction in blood cell counts, nausea, vomiting, diarrhea, stomach upset and irritation, itching rash, hair loss, dizziness, and increased susceptibility to infection.
>
> Less common side effects include . . . slight paralysis.[50]

Hausknecht selected women for the study who were in good health, emotionally stable, and less than sixty-three days into their pregnancy. He administered a dose of methotrexate intramuscularly, then five to seven days later administered misoprostol intravaginally. Out of 178 women, 153 aborted after the first dose of misoprostol. A second dose of misoprostol was administered to the remaining twenty-five women, and eighteen then aborted. Seven women needed suction curettage. Two researchers at the University of California in San Francisco have also tested Hausknecht's regimen on more than fifty women and plan to test a hundred more. However, one member of the research team warned that women should not try this method on their own, since "we can't say with certainty that this is safe."[51]

The question of safety aside, the new abortifacients and post-coital contraceptives bring with them the prospect of commercial exploitation. Although the drugs cost less than $10, Hausknecht charges $650 per patient for the entire treatment.[52] London clinics offer treatment with RU-486 to American women who are able to remain in England for a two-week follow-up—a condition that restricts the patient pool to those with enough money and leisure for such a prolonged stay. If the FDA would approve and regulate an abortifacient for the American market, it would do much to right the present inequalities in access to abortion.

Abortion Rights Mobilization, the group who sponsored Benten's challenge regarding the illegality of the import ban, has also been frustrated by the delay in approving RU-486. They have replicated and synthesized a duplicate medication and are ready to begin clinical trials. This "clone" has reportedly been used for over five years in China. Although all the physicians involved in this enterprise undoubtedly have women's safety and interest at heart, the extensive trials through which RU-486 has already gone make it the safest abortifacient now known.

But is it safer than a pregnancy? This is determined, in part, by the age and health of the woman. It is also influenced by where she lives. For very young women, women in poor health, or women in parts of the world where advanced medical technology is lacking, using RU-486 as an abortifacient may indeed be safer than carrying a child to term.

Not that RU-486 is a no-risk way to terminate a pregnancy. At least one woman has died from the procedure. But surgical abortions, even the legal kind, are also not entirely safe (although they are a good deal safer than nonlegal improvisations, such as coat hangers and knitting needles inserted through the cervix). RU-486 is at least as safe, and probably safer, than the chemical abortions that are currently obtainable in the American market and that are not as well supervised. Furthermore, if abortion itself is a matter of choice, so too, to a certain extent, should the method be, and RU-486 certainly ranks among the respectable options.

FDA approval of RU-486 may actually decrease the availability of surgical abortions. That is, many physicians may switch to RU-486 as their method of choice for terminating a pregnancy and discontinue or reduce their practice of surgical abortion. Unfortunately, this is already happening in response to the increased violence of antichoice activists at abortion facilities. In fact, only approximately one-fourth of physicians are even trained in surgical abortion procedures. Training is not required for board certification. The AMA has recently indicated that it may change this policy and require all physicians to be trained in surgical abortion. It is hoped that this move will make it more difficult for antiabortionists to target certain physicians.

In France, RU-486 has not diminished the availability of surgical abortion. Only approximately 30 percent of women who have abortions in France abort using RU-486, although 80 percent of those who are eligible to use RU-486 select it over surgical abortion. RU-486 may or may not reduce the number of physicians who offer surgical abortions but will likely increase the number who offer abortions in general. In a recent survey, three out of four obstetricians/gynecologists said they would include RU-486 in their repertoire of treatments if it were FDA approved. Making it more difficult to target abortion providers would hopefully decrease the harassment clients currently endure from antiabortionists.

Some argue that RU-486 will increase reliance on physicians, since it requires more visits than surgical abortion, and that the whole abortion process should be demedicalized. However, at this point, it is the medicalization of the process that imposes some regulation. Demedicalization could be a slippery slope whereby less credentialed individuals can offer cut-rate, lower-quality services.

Benefits of Approving RU-486

Perhaps the most appealing attribute of RU-486 is its potential for treating various illnesses. This is also likely to be the most profitable aspect of RU-486 for manufacturers. Several countries have already begun researching the drug's possibilities as a treatment for prostate, ovarian, and brain cancer, Parkinson's disease, glaucoma, Cushing's syndrome, depression, premenstrual syndrome, and Alzheimer's disease. In the United States, investigation into using RU-486 as a treatment for breast cancer, endometriosis, and fibroid tumors is currently under way. Progesterone, which is produced in both males and females, exacerbates a number of these illnesses, and a progesterone inhibitor such as RU-486 could attenuate them. For example, in meningiomas (benign brain tumors) symptoms worsen during pregnancy, when a woman produces greater amounts of progesterone.[53] RU-486 reduces the amount of progesterone that cells absorb and curtails the growth of the tumor. Unfortunately, the FDA ban has impeded American research on the therapeutic uses of RU-486 as well as on its contraceptive and abortifacient properties. It is ironic that "pro-life" forces, by threatening to boycott products from any manufacturer or distributor of RU-486, have helped to keep a potentially life-*saving* drug out of the hands of American researchers and consumers.

In addition to providing treatment for numerous disorders and ailments, RU-486 could ease the implementation of many obstetric/gynecological procedures. When used with synthetic prostaglandins, RU-486 seems to decrease pain during surgical abortions. In the case of a miscarriage, RU-486 can assist in expelling the dead fetus. Finally, RU-486 can facilitate the opening of the cervix in obstetric/gynecological procedures such as D & E.

If RU-486 is made available in the United States, researchers can at least begin to examine the drug's properties, even if not in the context of women's reproductive health. In addition, RU-486 may facilitate research and treatment of illnesses, such as breast and ovarian cancer, that are life-threatening to women. Moreover, the drug may provide new leads in treating some sources of infertility, such as fibroids and endometriosis. This may render other potentially dangerous procedures, performed to cure or circumvent infertility, unnecessary.

Finally, approval of RU-486 may make abortions more accessible to rural populations in the United States and third world countries. Worldwide, approximately five hundred women die *each day* from botched abortions. RU-486 could greatly diminish this number. Of course, RU-486 could potentially increase this number, if the drug has unknown long-term effects. But this is a moot point in countries where the average life span for women is already short. Regardless, it is unlikely that RU-486 could turn out to be as deadly, and on so wide a scale, as botched surgical abortions currently are. Although, the medical facilities and supervision in third world countries may not be adequate for administration of RU-486, neither are they adequate for surgical abortions.

If RU-486 became available in the United States, it would have a tremendous potential for abuse, ranging from a woman turning her prescription over to a friend if she decided to continue her pregnancy to physicians writing unmonitored prescriptions that could become black market drugs. In addition, if any physician could prescribe RU-486, it would be impossible to follow up on or track patients, especially if they failed to return for subsequent treatment. None of this has happened in France, where the drug is strictly regulated. The United States would have to implement a similar policy immediately upon approval of the drug. Other medical procedures, such as alternative insemination, illustrate the disastrous consequences that can attend the failure to regulate a reproduction "industry." Finally, it is essential that women be strongly encouraged to return for follow-up treatment.

Clearly, RU-486 is not a panacea. However, as with other reproductive technologies, it is here to stay. Now the emphasis should shift to regulation over, and research on, the processes and products of these technological developments.

Epilogue

On 30 December 1994, John C. Salvi III shot and killed the receptionists at two abortion clinics in Massachusetts. Salvi quietly walked into the first clinic and asked "Is this Planned Parenthood?" When Shannon Lowney said that it was, he opened fire with a .22-caliber rifle.

This brings the known death toll among abortion clinic workers to five. Two physicians and a security escort have also been killed while attempting to do their jobs. Scores of others have been injured and threatened. There have been kidnappings, arson, bombings, and violence. Some people believe that anti-abortion tactics have simply become another form of terrorism. After the violence in Massachusetts, almost everyone condemned Salvi's actions. Yet Planned Parenthood received one call with the message "You got what you deserved," and Salvi had supporters marching outside his jail cell.[54] Abortion remains the most emotionally charged political issue in the United States since the civil rights movement. Almost everyone has an opinion, usually a vehement and unequivocal one.

Baulieu, the drug researcher who synthesized RU-486, once commented, "In France, issues of morality tend to be individual, private matters. In the United States, they can turn into general political debates."[55] Certainly, when issues of morality concern women's reproductive rights, they frequently turn into general political debates.

[6]

Reproductive Interventions

ॐ

$\mathcal{A}$ngela was only thirteen years old when she was diagnosed with leukemia. For nearly a decade she battled the cancer, which cost her her left leg and hip. Finally, the cancer went into remission; Angela married and became pregnant. Unfortunately, the disease returned, and Angela, twenty-seven years old and six months pregnant, entered the hospital to die.

Aware that she would probably not carry the baby to term, Angela agreed to allow physicians to perform a cesarean section after the twenty-eighth week of her pregnancy, when the fetus might be viable, even though the surgery was likely to hasten her own death. Angela's condition rapidly deteriorated during the twenty-fifth and twenty-sixth weeks of her pregnancy, and it became clear that she might not survive until the twenty-eighth week. Furthermore, because of her condition, her physicians speculated that the fetus was being deprived of the oxygen crucial to normal development. They estimated that the fetus would have a 50 to 60 percent chance of survival, with a 20 percent chance of impairment, if an emergency cesarean section were performed immediately.

Angela was under heavy sedation, and it is unclear whether she was capable of giving an informed and clear-headed consent to the procedure. Apparently she consented at one point and denied consent at another. However, Angela's family clearly opposed the operation. They felt that she had endured enough pain. The hospital sought judicial intervention to determine their legal (and to a certain extent moral) responsibilities. Could they, and more importantly should they, force Angela to undergo a cesarean section to which she had not explicitly consented? Did the rights of the fetus override Angela's right to bodily integrity, her right to make decisions about what could be done to her own body, and even, perhaps, her right to life itself?

The court ordered the cesarean section be performed on Angela. As she was being taken to surgery, a panel of three appeals court judges upheld the decision. The baby died within hours, and Angela died two days later, with the knowledge that the surgery had been conducted without her explicit consent and that the baby had died. After Angela's death the decision was overturned, and her parents won a civil suit against the hospital. The court held that even when a patient is close to death, medical personnel must still abide by his or her wishes, unless a compelling reason to override them exists. Angela should have been allowed to make her own decisions about her life and health.

Unlike Angela, most women facing the possibility of cesarean section are in a state of mind where they are capable of clearly giving or withholding consent. However, like Angela, they may still find that the choice is taken out of their hands. During the 1960s and even into the 1970s, the chance that a pregnant woman in the United States would have a cesarean section was approximately 5 percent, or one in twenty. Today the probability is between 20 and 25 percent, one in five, or possibly even one in four.[1] Hospitals vary in their cesarean section rate, with some topping 50 percent. The rates also vary from state to state, ranging from 16.3 percent (Colorado) to 28.4 percent (Arkansas).[2] In fact, it has been predicted that if the trend continues unabated, the rate could reach 40 percent by the year 2000. In just two decades the rate has quadrupled.[3]

In a cesarean section the baby does not emerge through the vaginal canal but is removed from the uterus through surgery. After the woman has been prepped for surgery and catheterized, a regional or general anesthetic is administered. If regional, the woman may feel some uncomfortable pushing and pulling, although a screen generally prevents her from watching the procedure. If a general anesthetic is used, the woman is unconscious during the "birth." Horizontal incisions are made in the abdominal and uterine walls, and the placenta is "delivered." Then the uterus is lifted through the opening and sutured while resting on the woman's abdomen. After the uterus is returned, the woman is externally sutured with clamps or "staples." Generally an intravenous tube (IV) for nutrition and medication is used during the surgery and sometimes afterward. After several hours in the recovery room, the woman may be transferred to a postpartum room.

Women often experience pain, soreness, fatigue, and gas after a cesarean and may remain catheterized for a day or two. The hospital stay is usually three to four times longer than for a vaginal delivery. Overall recovery takes longer too, and the pain and weakness may continue for four to six weeks. The risk of hemorrhage and infection is enhanced, as are other complications associated with surgery, such as adverse reactions to the anesthesia, damage to the bowel, bladder, or other organs, chronic pain from scar tissue, infertility, and miscarriage. In general, the rate of complications for cesarean sections is five to ten times higher than for vaginal births.[4]

Cesarean sections are supposed to be reserved for high-risk births. For these births cesareans have probably increased the survival rate and/or decreased complications and impairments for both the mother and child. High-risk situations include cephalopelvic distortion (the fetus's head is too large to pass through the pelvis), a fetal or maternal condition that makes labor and vaginal delivery risky, unusual fetal presentation (e.g., breech), placenta previa (the placenta is blocking the cervical opening), or abruptio placenta (the placenta has partially separated from the uterine wall).[5] However, these maladies are not increasing at such an accelerated rate as to account for the tremendous rise in cesarean sections.

Given a choice, it is unlikely that most women would prefer a cesarean section over a vaginal delivery (although some do). Cesarean sections are not on the rise because women are clamoring to undergo an often unnecessary surgery that results in death two to five times as often as vaginal delivery does. Many women die every year from unnecessary cesareans. Ralph Nader's Public Citizen, a consumer research and advocacy group, estimates the optimal cesarean section rate at 12 percent; the United States Public Health service has set a nationwide goal of 15 percent by the year 2000.[6] But the cesarean rate continues to skyrocket, demonstrating once again how the failure to regulate a reproductive industry endangers the health of women.

The Rise in Cesarean Rates

Why has the cesarean section rate risen over the last three decades? Although the idea may seem counterintuitive, medical technology itself might be partially to blame. Electronic fetal monitors (EFMs), once reserved for high-risk births, are now used routinely (in three out of four births in 1990).[7] EFMs, which can alert physicians to the first indications of fetal distress, no matter how minute, come in two forms, external and internal. The external monitor is strapped on a woman's abdomen and detects fetal heartbeat and contractions through ultrasound. After labor has begun and the amniotic sac has ruptured, a sensor can be attached to the fetus's scalp to provide a more accurate measure of heart rate and pressure through internal monitoring. EFMs are highly unreliable, producing many false positives and often signaling distress when none exists. Unfortunately, once alerted, many physicians immediately resort to a cesarean section or other intervention without investigating the source, or even the reality, of the apparent distress. Two factors may contribute to this knee-jerk reaction.

First, obstetricians and gynecologists are among the physicians most often sued for malpractice in the United States, and more suits are won against them than against any other medical specialty. In part, this is due to the emotional investment of their patients. They are understandably cautious. An obstetrician is more likely to be sued for not performing a cesarean section than for performing one. A baby may suffer side effects from the anesthesia used during a cesarean or breathing problems from the lack of stimulation the lungs normally receive during a vaginal birth but runs a greater risk of damage or death if the cesarean is not performed than if it is.

Statistics support the theory that many cesareans are performed because the doctor fears being sued. In one study, white women had a higher cesarean rate than black women (23.6 percent versus 18.6 percent) and college-educated women a higher rate than high school dropouts (24.9 percent versus 18.5 percent).[8] It is reasonable to speculate that physicians anticipate more lawsuits from white women than from black and more from better educated women. Women with private insurance are also more likely to file a lawsuit than Medicaid recipients, and the former have a higher cesarean rate than the latter.

Second, the EFM has partially replaced the personnel who supervised the birth process in the past, personnel capable of exercising discretion that a machine cannot provide. Moreover, the human element may generate a level of comfort that relaxes both the woman and the fetus. In the Netherlands, using personnel rather than EFMs to assess the condition of the fetus has proven quite successful in keeping cesarean rates low (7.9 percent in 1991).[9] There pregnant women are divided into high- and low-risk groups, and those in the latter are attended by midwives and general practitioners during labor. In the United States, some women have been hiring labor assistants, or "doulas," who provide emotional support during delivery. Other labor assistants, known as "monitrices," go beyond emotional support and may perform vaginal exams, take blood pressure, and monitor the fetal heartbeat. Women with labor assistants tend to have shorter labor, fewer cesarean sections and require less anesthetic and fewer inductions. In one South African study, women with doulas were found to be less anxious about their baby the day after birth and, six weeks later, experienced less postpartum depression and had more positive self-esteem regarding their capacities as mothers.[10]

Deliveries assisted or performed by midwives also have many of these benefits. Midwives may work with women in hospitals or at home. On the whole, midwives employ noninterventionist techniques in their practices, attempting natural solutions before resorting to medical ones. However, midwives, particularly those that assist in home births, are being increasingly forced by state regulations to have a nursing degree in order to become licensed. Even if they do become licensed, they may not receive support for their practice from other obstetric professionals. For example, in 1975, Yale University Hospital withdrew the rights of physicians or nurse-midwives who participated in home births to practice in the hospital.

Of course, providing every pregnant women with a midwife, labor assistant, or nurse would require an increase in personnel, and most insurers will not cover such "luxuries." Insurance companies often neglect prevention at the expense of later intervention, proving themselves penny-wise but pound-foolish. Eliminating half the cesarean sections performed in the United States per year could save approximately $1.3 billion in health care costs.

Profit has been suggested as another reason that cesarean rates have been rising. The average hospital and physician cost for a vaginal delivery in 1991 was $4,720, while the average cesarean section cost $7,826. In 1993, 19.5 percent of pregnant women on Medicaid underwent cesareans, while the figures for women covered through private insurance or Blue Cross/Blue Shield were 25.7 and 26.7 percent, respectively. This differential is surprising, given that it is the Medicaid recipients who would ostensibly be most likely to have the kind of poor prenatal care and pregnancy complications that make cesarean section necessary. However, Medicaid offers little monetary incentive to perform a cesarean, while private insurance is more generous. Women who self-paid had the lowest cesarean rate of all (16.1 percent). Additionally, government and teaching hospitals, which provide little financial incentive for cesareans, have lower cesarean rates. Nonprofit hospitals had a rate of 22 percent, as opposed to 29 percent for proprietary hospitals.

The influence of the profit motive is also suggested by research results on repeat cesareans. For-profit hospitals had higher rates of repeat cesareans than Kaiser-Permanente health maintenance organizations, whose physicians are encouraged to keep costs down.[11] Contrary to popular wisdom, it is possible for a woman who has had a cesarean to have a vaginal birth in subsequent pregnancies (a VBAC—vaginal birth after cesarean). The notion that this is impossible led many physicians to routinely schedule cesareans for pregnant women who had previously had one, a practice that contributed to the exploding cesarean rate. Initially, when vertical incisions were used for cesareans, physicians feared that a subsequent vaginal birth might rupture the uterus. Today, horizontal incisions are the norm, and about one-third of the women who have given birth through cesarean section proceed to vaginal deliveries in subsequent pregnancies. The possibility of a rupture of the uterus is less than 1 percent. Even so with modern obstetric technology a rupture rarely causes a problem. In fact, the VBAC rate increased from 12.6 percent in 1988 to 25.4 percent in 1993. Ideally, it could climb even higher.

Insurance companies seem to be attempting to squelch any profit motive connected with the performance of c-sections. For example, in Illinois, preferred providers of Blue Cross make the same amount regardless of whether the delivery was vaginal or cesarean.[12] Insurance companies have also attempted to educate pregnant employees and their partners about the benefits of vaginal delivery and the drawbacks of cesareans. Some insurance companies are even willing to pay for a second opinion regarding scheduled cesareans, in order to decrease unnecessary surgeries.

Cigna Health Plan has taken a different approach. Instead of restricting the physician's profit, they have decided to restrict the patient's care. A memo sent to Florida obstetricians indicated that women who give birth through cesarean section were to be discharged within forty-eight hours, within twenty-four if the delivery was vaginal.[13] This approach is not unique to Cigna. Whereas the average hospital stay after a vaginal delivery was 3.9 days in 1970, it is now down to two days, with some women being discharged within eight hours. Reduction in the amount of hospital time that insurers will cover does not penalize physicians, because their fee is largely for the delivery. It does hurt hospitals somewhat, but mainly it hurts women and their infants. Although a quick discharge may reduce the possibility of babies being exposed to infections at the hospital and may actually facilitate bonding between mother and child, many mothers, particularly first-timers, are not ready for discharge so quickly. Hospitals are now experiencing an upswing in admissions of jaundiced and dehydrated babies whose mothers did not realize that their milk was not being properly released. However, through implementing such managed-care policies, insurers stand to save $4 billion per year: $1000 for each day that a maternity room is not used.

In response to these "drive-through deliveries," the American Academy of Pediatrics has issued a policy statement indicating that most mothers and babies need to stay in the hospital at least forty-eight hours after delivery. In addition, several states have implemented laws requiring insurers to pay for a minimum of forty-eight hours of hospital care for both the mother and the baby. (This is reduced to twenty-four hours if insurers will pay for a follow-up home visit from a nurse.) Two other states have enacted similar laws, and several more are proposing them. On 11 May 1996, the day before Mother's Day, President Clinton joined in the fray and appealed to Congress to enact a law that would guarantee women a forty-eight-hour hospital stay after a vaginal delivery, ninety-six hours after a cesarean.

Some physicians may favor cesareans for another reason: convenience. The physician's investment of time is generally *less* for a cesarean section than for a vaginal delivery. In fact, for a scheduled cesarean, the delivery date is arranged prior to labor. The recent trend toward inducing labor when a woman is "overdue" also suggests a convenience motive. It is impossible to determine scientifically if convenience is a factor in the rising cesarean rate, but it is disheartening to think that some physicians may prescribe cesareans or inductions simply to make their schedules more agreeable and without regard for the patient's distress.

Some medical professionals have suggested that additional reasons underlie the rising cesarean rate. They contend that women are gaining more weight during pregnancy, making it difficult to deliver the larger babies vaginally. While it is true that women are gaining more weight during pregnancy now than they did in the past (when physicians encouraged only twelve to fifteen pounds of weight gain during pregnancy), this factor alone cannot account for the cesarean boom. The tendency toward weight gain during pregnancy is presumably nationwide, but cesarean rates vary greatly among states and hospitals. Additionally, if bigger babies necessitate cesarean sections, then why aren't physicians forestalling excessive weight gain by educating and monitoring their patients rather than intervening surgically at the last minute?

Many physicians also argue that the cesarean rate has risen because technology has enabled more high-risk women to become pregnant and give birth. This is true, but other industrialized countries have not seen similar astronomical increases in cesarean rates. Japan, Slovenia, and the former Czechoslovakian republic have cesarean rates of 6 to 7 percent;[14] Britain, 13 percent.[15] In addition, the heavy reliance on cesarean section has not lowered the rate of infant death in the United States. Perhaps that is why so many voices, from the U.S. Department of Public Health to the American College of Obstetricians and Gynecologists, are calling for a reduction in cesareans. Yet researchers concentrate their efforts on creating more high-risk technology to impregnate women rather than on investigating ways to facilitate the birth process.

Whose Life Is This Anyway?

In an innovative move to both increase the accountability of physicians and protect them against lawsuits, Florida has enacted legislation requiring that they follow guidelines regarding cesareans if federal or state money is used in any way as payment for the surgery: "These practice parameters shall address, at a minimum, the following: feasibility of attempting a vaginal delivery for each patient with a prior caesarean section; dystocia, including arrested dilation and prolonged deceleration phase; fetal distress; and fetal malposition."[16] This legislation also requires that hospitals establish peer review boards to assess whether each cesarean conducted was in fact necessary. The results of each review are shared with the physician and used as part of the hospital's quality assurance monitoring. The overall results are then made available to the governor, the Speaker of the Florida House of Representatives, and the president of the Florida Senate. This legislation represents a step in the right direction. However, it does not apply to cesareans covered by private insurance, which are the ones that most need monitoring.

The judicial system has also become involved in forced medical reproductive interventions. Angela's case was probably the most famous instance of an enforced cesarean, but it was not an isolated one. Many other women have been coerced into cesareans they did not want.

A Nigerian woman, name unknown, pregnant with triplets, refused to consent to a cesarean although the doctor recommended that such a delivery would be safer for the multiple births. This woman believed that a natural delivery would be safe for her. In addition, she and her husband planned to return to Africa, to an area where cesarean delivery might not be possible should they have children later. . . . The hospital obtained a court order to perform a cesarean, but the woman was not told of it until she went into labor. When she and her husband resisted, seven security officers forced the husband from the hospital. The woman was tied to the bed while struggling and screaming and a forced cesarean was performed. The woman and the three infants survived the surgery.[17]

Prior to Angela's case, judicial response to such situations was mixed. Some courts would order the woman to undergo a cesarean while others would not. Now many courts have chosen to follow the precedent set by Angela's case. It is impossible to determine how many women have been forced to undergo cesareans by court order and have not appealed the decision or how many women have conceded to the operation when threatened with a court order.

Pregnant women have also been forced to undergo blood transfusions, to deliver in a hospital rather than at home, and to remain in the hospital because they did not follow medical advice. Many states have laws that force a pregnant woman in a terminal condition to remain on life support, *even if she has a living will specifically stipulating that such measures should not be used to keep her alive.* In each of these instances, the health, welfare, and rights of the fetus supersede the health, welfare, and rights of the pregnant woman.

So Now What?

As physicians began to take over the childbirth process from midwives over a century ago, it became increasingly subject to technological intervention. No longer were women giving birth in the quiet privacy of their homes but rather in sterile examination rooms with bright lights; anesthesia dulled pain but eventually led to the use of forceps to compensate for the inability of the anesthetized mother to push. In the last few decades, with the help of women's health advocates, many physicians have begun to realize the benefits of *not* intervening, and look with favor on birthing rooms, natural childbirth, and the methods of Lamaze. But, ironically, the rate for the most invasive intervention, the cesarean section, continues high.

The medical profession is beginning to police itself with regard to cesareans, but government drags its feet. While legislatures have been quick to regulate midwives (thereby decreasing the options available to pregnant women outside of hospitals) and have not hesitated to reach for control over the lives and choices of pregnant women, legislation to protect pregnant women from the excesses of industries like the medical profession is slow and underinclusive. The judicial system has compounded this problem by not taking a definitive stand on constitutional rights related to bodily integrity.

Finally, although childbirth is one of the most common events to occur in hospitals, it is still one of the least understood. The medical profession has done very little to further its understanding of childbirth and develop more options for problem pregnancies and have indeed shown little interest in doing so. In some ways it is the "everyday" quality of childbirth that discourages investigation: it is taken for granted and seems to offer few enticing prospects for research. But since physicians themselves have made the process more complicated, they should feel obligated to find better solutions, if not to all problems, at least to the problems they have helped to create.

Other Unnecessary Reproductive Surgeries

Approximately one hundred years ago, physicians began performing "cesarean hysterectomies." It was believed that women would die 95 percent of the time from a cesarean unless the uterus was also removed. Removing the uterus presumably reduced fatality to 5 percent.[18]

Although these procedures are rarely performed together today, they still keep pace with each other. Cesarean section is the most frequently performed surgery in the United States; next in line is hysterectomy. Approximately 600,000 hysterectomies are performed in the United States each year, at a cost of roughly $2 billion. Of that number, 76.4 percent are performed on women of childbearing age (between twenty and forty-nine years old). Therefore, a significant percentage of women living in the United States will probably face a decision about surgery on their reproductive organs at some time in their life, whether it is a cesarean or a hysterectomy.

The similarities between cesareans and hysterectomies do not end there. Women's health advocates, medical professionals, insurance companies, consumer groups, and patients have been questioning the necessity of hysterectomies for decades.

> As long ago as 1948, documented evidence indicated that hysterectomy was an over-performed operation. By the late 1960's the emerging women's movement helped to focus national attention on the subject, and in 1978, hysterectomy, along with tonsillectomy, became the central issue in a congressional hearing on unnecessary surgery in the U.S. The hearing brought to light the fact that there had been no well-designed studies to determine the appropriate indications for either operation, then the two most commonly performed surgical procedures.[19]

A large-scale clinical study was conducted on tonsillectomies, and the procedure was determined to be largely unnecessary. The incidence of the operation subsequently decreased. No comparable study has ever been conducted on hysterectomies. However, a widely cited 1990 Blue Cross/Blue Shield of Illinois survey suggests that at least one-third of hysterectomies are unnecessary. Blue Cross/Blue Shield would, of course, benefit from a reduction in the number of hysterectomies and its findings might be suspected of bias on that account. But disinterested researchers have also estimated the number of unnecessary hysterectomies to be very high, sometimes as high as 90 percent.[20] Even if the figure is only 30 percent, at the current rate of 600,000 hysterectomies per year, with one death for every thousand, unnecessary hysterectomy would account for 180 deaths per year.

Kinds and Causes of Hysterectomy

There are four basic types of hysterectomy. A *partial* or *subtotal hysterectomy* involves only the removal of the uterus. In a *complete* or *total abdominal hysterectomy* the cervix is also removed. A *total abdominal hysterectomy with bilateral salpingo-oophorectomy* includes removal of the uterus, cervix, ovaries, and fallopian tubes. Removing the ovaries alone is termed an oophorectomy. Finally, in a *radical hysterectomy,* the uterus, cervix, ovaries, fallopian tubes, upper portions of the vagina, and pelvic lymph nodes are excised.

All of these surgeries can be conducted abdominally, through an incision in the abdominal and uterine walls. It is also possible to conduct some of these surgeries vaginally, reducing recovery time and expense. However, only about one in five hysterectomies are vaginal.

Most hysterectomies are elective surgeries, performed under nonemergency conditions. Over time, individual physicians and the medical profession as a whole have found hundreds of reasons for recommending a hysterectomy, including "overeating, painful menstruation, attempted suicide, and, most particularly, masturbation, erotic tendencies or promiscuity."[21] Currently, the most common reason (30 percent) is fibroid tumors. Fibroid tumors are benign growths present in 30 to 50 percent of women between forty and fifty years old. African-American women are particularly susceptible. It is believed that fibroids may be related to estrogen levels, since they seem to be nonexistent prior to puberty, shrink after menopause, and worsen during pregnancy. Fibroids are generally inside the endometrium (the lining of the uterus) or within or outside the uterine wall. They vary in size and number and may or may not induce symptoms, such as bleeding, pain, pressure, and infertility.

The next most common reason for recommending a hysterectomy (24 percent) is endometriosis. Although endometriosis was described over a century ago, it still remains an elusive disorder, in which part of the endometrium, normally shed at the start of each menstrual cycle, has migrated instead to other areas of the body. One theory suggests that endometriosis begins with retrograde menstruation, that is, when the menstrual fluid that is usually shed through the cervix is forced back up through the uterus and sometimes out the oviducts. Retrograde menstruation probably occurs in most women without causing endometriosis. However, in some women, the tissue implants itself and begins to grow. Generally this endometrial tissue remains within the pelvic area, but it has been known to travel anywhere in the body, including the limbs and major organs. The implants may bleed cyclically with the menstrual cycle, or the tissue may rupture, causing internal bleeding. The tissue may even develop into benign tumors. The primary symptoms of endometriosis are cramping and pain, although some women experience neither. For those who do experience pain, it may occur during menstruation or intercourse or both. During menstruation some women may also suffer from nausea, vomiting, heavy bleeding, fainting, headaches, and diarrhea. A few women may experience abdominal bleeding or infertility.

The third most common reason for a hysterectomy (20 percent) is a prolapse. A prolapse occurs when weakened ligaments enable the uterus and/or cervix to descend into the vagina. In rare cases, the prolapse may even protrude from the body. Prolapse may cause pelvic pain or backache, frequent bladder infections, or a feeling of fullness or incontinence due to pressure on the bladder or bowel. Interestingly some physicians have "induced" prolapses in an attempt to "help" women.

> Twenty-five years ago, we often used mild prolapse of the uterus to justify a hysterectomy to a hospital committee that would otherwise have required a woman to have as many as six children before she could be sterilized. We'd place an instrument on her cervix, and attempt to pull it down into the vagina so as to be able to say that she had a so-called uterine prolapse with traction. Fortunately, these tactics are considered to be unnecessary and unethical today, when no woman should have a hysterectomy suggested to her solely for sterilization purposes. (Although unfortunately, some of these practices still continue!) In actual fact, very few women—even those who do have legitimate prolapse—require hysterectomy today.[22]

Some states now have legislation against performing hysterectomies for purposes of sterilization. The physicians who "induced" these prolapses apparently had altruistic motives. But the patriarchal notion that they knew what was best for the patient, with or without consulting her, is objectionable, as it is in medical practice generally and in obstetrics and gynecology in particular.

Other reasons physicians have recommended a hysterectomy include abnormal bleeding and, of course, cancer.[23] Abnormal bleeding in and of itself does not justify a hysterectomy. After all, most women do not know the actual range of "normal" menstrual bleeding. "Normal" flow varies from individual to individual and across the life span, usually increasing and decreasing several times in the course of a woman's life. However, most physicians accept their patient's self report of flow without attempting any objective assessment. Before performing a hysterectomy for abnormal bleeding, it is important to assess whether in fact the bleeding is abnormal and if so, what is causing it. Uterine cancer, hormonal imbalances, fibroids, and estrogen replacement therapy are all associated with abnormal uterine bleeding. It is not even necessarily a sign of gynecological malfunction but may spring from other problems altogether. Numerous women have undergone a hysterectomy for abnormal bleeding only to discover later that they had a completely benign condition.

One out of ten hysterectomies is performed with cancer treatment or cancer prevention in mind, clearly the most legitimate reason. However, the justification for hysterectomy as prevention or treatment depends on the type of cancer involved. The most common gynecological malignancy is cancer of the uterus, followed by cancer of the cervix, followed by ovarian cancer. Other gynecological cancers do occur, such as vaginal, vulvar, or fallopian, but not nearly as often.

One out of every forty-five girls born today will eventually battle uterine cancer, usually of the endometrium. It is generally detected at around the time of menopause or later. However, women who are at risk for developing endometrial cancer can be routinely screened through an endometrial biopsy. If the disease is detected in its early stages, alternatives to hysterectomy, such as hormonal therapy, are often successful. In an advanced stage, some type of hysterectomy is usually required.

Women are encouraged to have a regular Pap smear every year to facilitate early detection of cervical cancer, a disease that strikes one in every sixty-three women and particularly targets women of lower socioeconomic status. As with uterine abnormalities, depending upon the severity of the disease, a hysterectomy may not be necessary, for cervical cancer spreads slowly. However, once invasive cancer of the cervix has been established, hysterectomy may be unavoidable.

Very few women will actually have ovarian cancer during their lives: about twenty-one thousand cases are diagnosed in the United States each year. It is however the most deadly of the gynecological cancers, due partly to the fact that it is so difficult to detect and treat. The symptoms are vague and can be misinterpreted. As with the other gynecological cancers, treatment depends on the extent of the disease.

Sometimes physicians will remove healthy ovaries from a woman to prevent the *possibility* of ovarian cancer. Healthy ovaries are removed in 60 percent of women who have abdominal hysterectomies. In women under forty-five years old who have hysterectomies because of fibroids, 37 percent lose healthy ovaries. But the incidence of ovarian cancer is so low that the ovaries of fifteen hundred women would have to be removed to prevent one case of ovarian cancer (barring an overwhelming hereditary tendency in any particular case). There is little justification for the "preventative" removal of gynecological structures.

Imagine an often cited parallel. Prostate cancer strikes five out of every hundred males, but removal of the prostate can significantly impair male sexual function. Would any physician suggest removing the prostates of twenty males to prevent cancer in one of them? When the ovaries are removed, the woman is sent into an early menopause and may be plagued with a variety of side effects. In fact, the side effects of hysterectomy differ radically depending upon whether the ovaries remain intact.

Surgical Complications and Side Effects

It is difficult to determine what percentage of women suffer surgical complications or side effects from hysterectomy. Many women may not report complications or side effects because they are embarrassed or are not aware that they are experiencing a side effect of the surgery. Too often physicians and patients dismiss complaints as psychological disturbances unrelated to surgery. Therefore, any estimate of the number of women suffering complications or side effects of hysterectomy is likely to err on the low side. Nevertheless, one often cited statistic indicates that nearly 50 percent of women suffer complications.[24]

The most frequent complication is infection, which afflicts approximately one out of every three women. Other complications include hemorrhage, damage to surrounding organs (particularly the bowel and bladder), the need for additional surgery, transfusion reactions, cardiac arrest, problems with clotting, stroke, difficulty with incision healing, incisional or instrumental hernia, anesthesia complications, and death. Some of these complications are rare; some are relatively frequent.[25]

It is impossible to list all the potential side effects from a hysterectomy. Perhaps the most far-reaching side effects are those that touch on subjective well-being and quality of life. Ironically, many women experience a decrease in quality of life after hysterectomy, when it was the potential increase that convinced them to undergo the surgery in the first place. Although some women report increased anxiety and irritability following a hysterectomy, the most widely reported side effect is depression. In some women the depression is transient; in others it is long-term and may even be linked to suicide. The depression could stem from any number of causes, including hormonal changes (as with postpartum depression), physical changes, unsuccessful remediation of symptoms, or loss of reproductive organs.

Some women report a diminished sexual capacity after hysterectomy. Although the effect of hysterectomy on sexuality has not been well researched, it appears that surgery does have an effect on pleasure and libido.

> It isn't surprising that since 1944, only fourteen studies have been published on the sexual impact of hysterectomy. However, the results of these few studies suggest that hysterectomy does have a negative impact on women's sex lives. All but one found some evidence of diminished desire or lessened (or lack of) orgasm. On the average, more than one-third of all women questioned reported a change for the worse in sexual feelings.[26]

Women who have had their ovaries removed are more likely to express dissatisfaction with their sexual encounters, especially if hormone replacement therapy has not been initiated. (In hormone replacement therapy, women are provided with synthetic hormones that simulate natural hormonal functioning.)

The physical side effects of hysterectomy can include fatigue, insomnia, weight gain, headaches, dizziness, backaches, vaginal dryness, "hot flashes," and an increase in bladder or bowel problems. If the ovaries have been removed, more serious consequences can result. The body abruptly ceases to produce hormones that the ovaries helped to regulate, the lack of which has been linked to an increased susceptibility to heart disease and osteoporosis. Overall, women are at a much greater risk for heart disease and osteoporosis than for ovarian cancer, so removing healthy ovaries to prevent the latter seems ill judged.

Some of the most devastating consequences of hysterectomy occur when women awaken to find that the surgery has been more extensive than they were led to expect. Patients sometimes sign blanket consent forms that allow physicians to remove any organ they deem necessary to remove. Sometimes these forms do allow patients to specify which organs they do not want removed. However, such a selection may overreach the patient's knowledge. For example, in England one physician was investigated for aborting a fetus during a hysterectomy. The patient, who had endometriosis and had been trying to conceive, agreed to a hysterectomy after she was told that conception would be impossible. Her physician assured her that she could not be pregnant. During surgery, the physician discovered that she was, but the fetus was aborted with the removal of the uterus. The patient would not have consented to hysterectomy if she had known she was pregnant. Criminal charges were filed against the physician.

In another British case, a patient explicitly stated that she did not want her healthy ovary removed, but the physician removed it anyway. One Canadian woman received fifty-three thousand dollars in damages when her ovary was removed by surgical error. Her attorney complained that this was too little, given that, in another case, a man had received eighty thousand dollars when his testicle was mistakenly removed. Nora Coffey, director of HERS (Hysterectomy Educational Resources and Services Foundation), has indicated that such unauthorized removals are commonplace in the United States as well. To prevent such incidents, some states have enacted legislation requiring that patients be informed of all risks and sign a detailed consent prior to surgery.

In New York, patients must be provided with a standardized written summary that includes the diagnoses for which hysterectomy is typically a treatment, the types of hysterectomy, the side effects, and a discussion of alternative treatments. In California, patients must also receive information regarding the length and cost of the hospital stay. Each patient must also sign an informed consent prior to surgery; in California if the physician proceeds without obtaining such a consent, he or she is considered guilty of unprofessional conduct. Such legislation protects both patient and physician, but as yet the other forty-eight states have not followed suit.

Alternatives

The alternatives to hysterectomy vary according to the complaint. One current treatment for fibroids involves using antihormone agents, thereby decreasing the woman's estrogen levels and shrinking the tumors. If a woman is in her late forties, this may slow the growth of the tumors enough so that the natural processes of menopause can be relied upon to do the rest. If the woman is younger, or the fibroids are particularly extensive, antihormone therapy may reduce the size of the tumors enough so that they can be removed through a procedure known as a myomectomy. In a myomectomy, the tumors are removed but the uterus remains intact, thus preserving fertility.

Since the mid-1980s two types of endoscopes have made it possible to perform myomectomies less invasively, resulting in lower costs and shorter recoveries. Endoscopes are instruments with thin fiberoptic tubes that are inserted into the body and act as telescopes, transmitting internal images to a video monitor. Some endoscopes act solely to assist visualization, while others also have surgical functions. One type of endoscope, the hysteroscope, is inserted through the cervix. In a hysteroscopic myomectomy, electrical current or laser beams are used to cut fibroids from the uterine wall. If the fibroid is outside of the uterus, another type of endoscope, known as a laparoscope, can be inserted through an incision near the navel. Other small incisions in the abdominal wall assist in the myomectomy. Laparoscopes are also used to perform vaginal hysterectomies.

There are alternative treatments for endometriosis as well, including drug therapy. Physicians have also been performing a procedure known as dilation and curettage or D & C (often "jokingly" referred to as "dusting & cleaning") on women for years as a treatment for endometriosis. In a D & C the cervix is dilated and the lining of the uterus is gently scraped away using a sharp, spoon-shaped instrument (a curette). This procedure was common in the past and is still widely practiced today. The use of a hysteroscope could greater enhance its effectiveness, since it would make the interior of the uterus visible. In a variation of the D & C, termed endometrial ablation, the lining of the uterus is cut away through the use of laser beams or electrical current, with the assistance of a hysteroscope. Although more precise than a D & C, this procedure almost always results in infertility. Another therapy for endometriosis is tubal ligation. By tying the fallopian tubes, menstrual fluids are blocked from backing up into the pelvic cavity, making it difficult for endometrial tissue to travel and implant there. Needless to say, the passage of the egg to the uterus is also blocked, so pregnancy is unlikely.

Even prolapse can be treated through procedures other than hysterectomy. The ligaments supporting the uterus can be strengthened through exercise. In another minimally invasive procedure, a rubber or plastic pessary can be used to hold the uterus in place. Finally, it is possible to surgically realign the uterus, particularly with the aid of a laparoscope.

Despite numerous benefits, these alternative procedures are still used relatively seldom and often incorrectly. Hysterectomies are easier to perform and generally less time-consuming. Moreover, physicians are not routinely trained in the use of alternatives, particularly those that involve the use of endoscopes for gynecological procedures. These precision instruments require expert visual-motor coordination and a great deal of practice.

The procedures must be performed many times (at least twenty-five) before the physician can be considered adequately trained. Unfortunately, many physicians have no formal training with endoscopes or laparoscopes but learn, so to speak, on the job. Since it is so easy to perforate the uterus or surrounding organs with this technology, it is not surprising that there are many reports of more serious complications, including death, from endoscopically assisted gynecological procedures than from traditional hysterectomies. Once again, lack of regulation has resulted in women being used as guinea pigs. This is a perfect example of how technology could benefit women but does not, due to a lack of control over both the procedure and the provider.

As with cesareans, it is impossible to ignore the profit motive involved in hysterectomy. Fewer hysterectomies are performed when physicians are not directly compensated for the procedure, as with prepaid health plans (except in training hospitals where unnecessary hysterectomies have been performed to give interns practice in the procedure). Additionally, alternative procedures provide less financial incentive because they are time consuming.

Insurance plays an important part in the profit motive. On the one hand, some insurance companies have supported the performance of hysterectomies, since the operation will likely reduce the number of subsequent gynecological claims from the patient. On the other hand, other insurance companies are beginning to realize that they are paying for a vast amount of unnecessary surgery.

In order to reduce the number of unnecessary hysterectomies, insurance companies have implemented several new strategies. Some companies now require a second opinion. Others refuse to cover elective hysterectomies. Some innovative insurance companies meet with physicians who have high hysterectomy rates and discuss how his/her rates compare with those of other physicians, thus applying what might be considered peer pressure with educational overtones. In an extension of this procedure, one insurance company identifies communities with high rates of hysterectomy and implements review procedures. This company also rewards high-quality care (measured by low incidence of complications) with bonuses.

None of the alternatives presented is a panacea, and each has its own potential side effects and complications. Even so, hysterectomy should be the last, not the first, recourse for treating gynecological disorders. Unfortunately, the alternatives have not inspired, as one would expect, a significant and steady decline in the number of hysterectomies.

Interestingly, if anyone has begun to regulate the medical profession, it is the insurance industry, and the medical profession has fought this every step of the way. (Its response to managed care is just one example of this resistance.) But while women may benefit from some of the insurance companies' provisions and regulations, the companies clearly are not motivated by humanitarian concerns but by efforts to reduce expenditure.

Why Is Hysterectomy a First Choice and Not a Last Resort?

Many medical personnel persist in believing that the uterus is a disposable organ, even a nuisance, in the postchildbearing years. Castration is defined as removal of the sex glands (the ovaries or the testes). Would 600,000 men a year (76.4 percent of them still in their childbearing years) be recommended for, or consent to, testicular castration?

Most physicians and endocrinologists clearly do not understand the repercussions of hysterectomy, largely because they do not understand the effects of hormones and hormone changes.

Premenstrual syndrome, postpartum depression, even pregnancy symptoms—the medical profession clearly does not understand any of these conditions and has relegated them to the realm of psychology. In fact, although medical students are in general taught to look for a physical, not a psychological, basis for symptoms, the reverse is true when it comes to women's issues. Premenstrual syndrome now appears in the *Diagnostic and Statistical Manual of Mental Disorders*. Postpartum depression is not even covered in the curricula of most medical schools. When a woman balks at having her uterus removed, physicians often maintain that she is just being sentimental about her reproductive organs or suffering from "empty nest syndrome." However, this highlights an interesting disparity. If all of these disorders are simply psychological, why do physicians continue to treat them medically? If PMS is just a mental condition, then why prescribe everything from painkillers to hysterectomy for it?

The number of hysterectomies performed is also influenced by training and community norms. In other countries the hysterectomy rates are almost always less than the rate in the United States, sometimes as much as 50 percent less, yet the rates of death from gynecological disease are equal to that of the United States. In other words, American doctors are not in fact saving lives in proportion to the number of hysterectomies they perform, from which it is reasonable to conclude that many of these hysterectomies are unnecessary. More evidence of community influence comes from comparing regional rates within the United States. Like the rate of cesarean section, the rate of hysterectomy (among younger women) is higher in the South.[27] It is difficult to imagine that southern women actually have more gynecological problems that require cesareans and hysterectomies than do women elsewhere in the country. More likely, local norms affect the way a physician is trained and the way he or she evaluates and treats a patient's condition.

At present, cesarean section and hysterectomy, the two most common surgeries in the country, appear to protect physicians from liability more than they protect women's health and quality of life. The lack of understanding, lack of control or regulation over the process, and lack of investigation into alternatives is pervasive and appalling. Some physicians have begun to raise questions about these surgeries, to monitor themselves, and to seek alternatives, but they are in the minority, and the curricula of medical schools have not shown any significant corresponding change. Given how training and community norms affect medical decisions, a significant downward trend in the near future is unlikely. In the meantime, only the insurance companies are insisting on restraint.

Although it seems reasonable to suggest that women educate themselves on issues of reproductive health and become wiser consumers, not all women have the time, energy, and resources to do so. Moreover, some women are admitted for treatment in emergency situations and have no opportunity to study the issues before they are asked to make crucial decisions (or before others make these decisions on their behalf). The bottom line is that consumers pay professionals to know their area of expertise and to provide sound, reliable advice that has the consumer's best interest at heart. Physicians in particular are bound to honor the implicit contract, for they take an oath, which patients trust, to do no harm.

[7]

Back to the Future?

∞

*T*he Constitution guarantees certain rights to all citizens of the United States, regardless of gender. Many of these rights have been discussed in this book. Yet men and women are often treated quite differently, by the law, the medical profession, and society in general, when they try to exercise these rights, and taken as a whole, the disparities seem formidable. It is clear that "rights" are meaningless unless they are upheld by the legal system, and upheld for everyone.

All reproductive rights are inextricably linked, and losses in any one area may represent losses across the board. For example, if the state can pass laws forbidding pregnant women from using substances that may harm the fetus, what will happen to a woman's right to choose an abortion? Reproductive issues represent a complex array; none of them can be viewed in isolation.

These issues are only likely to become more complicated in

the future. Each year reproductive technologies sound more and more like science fiction. It is already possible to create identical twins by cloning a fertilized egg before it begins to subdivide. Researchers have also begun to successfully ovarian graft. With ovarian grafting, it may one day be possible to remove ovaries and cryopreserve them for future use by the woman or a donor. Thus, if a woman was undergoing chemotherapy or wanted to delay childbirth, she could preserve her ovaries until she was ready to use them, thereby retaining the integrity of the eggs. The reproductive technology "business" is already booming, and advances such as ovarian grafting will surely generate more interest and more business. In addition, recent judicial decisions, such as those regarding Baby Jessica and Baby Richard have made some couples leery of adopting and inclined to try for biological parenthood, no matter what the cost, effort, or risk.

Correspondingly, legal dilemmas have also become more complicated. Consider the case of Judith Hart. Judith was born in June 1991, although her biological father had died in June 1990. Judith's father, Edward, had semen specimens frozen prior to his death. His widow, Nancy, underwent GIFT after his death and conceived Judith. After Judith was born, Nancy applied to Social Security for survivor benefits for her but was denied. It seems Louisiana has a law stating that a child born more than three hundred days after a man's death cannot be his child. Should Judith be allocated survivor benefits? Should sperm or eggs be allowed to survive the individual from whom they came, or should they be destroyed upon his or her death? Reproductive technology is evolving so rapidly that it is reshaping society in ways that present conundrums on a daily basis.

As for substance abuse and pregnancy, new drugs are continually introduced into the American market, creating new opportunities for abuse and addiction. The funding for the "war on drugs" is largely allocated toward enforcement of laws rather than toward prevention. As Democrats and Republicans fight over who can cut more money from the federal budget, the minuscule amount of money available for prevention and treatment of addiction has dwindled. It is likely that most programs for pregnant substance abusers will be funded through private sources, since pregnant substance abusers represent only a small subset of the nation's drug abusers and legislators and politicians do not feel that a special outlay is warranted. Such shortsightedness is incredible, given the money that is eventually saved by effective preventative treatment. Moreover, as the number of pregnant women brought to court for substance abuse during pregnancy mounts, other pregnant substance abusers become more likely to avoid treatment centers out of fear of incarceration or of losing their children.

As for the workplace, it is not likely to spontaneously become safer for pregnant women. We need more intensive research into potential hazards. Again, this simply is not happening on a large enough scale or at a rapid enough pace to keep up with technological advances.

Abortion rights continue to remain on shaky ground. RU-486 trials have begun in the United States, but the journey from trials to FDA approval is a long and treacherous one. In the meantime politics or experimental setbacks could stall the project, and changing presidential administrations could stifle approval altogether. Even if RU-486 is made available, the abortion controversy will only shift to other arenas, not fade away.

Finally, cesarean and hysterectomy rates are not dramatically decreasing, and no one is systematically investigating the situation to determine how often and when these surgeries are actually necessary. Changes are unlikely without regulation, which is unlikely without research data. In the meantime, liability suits ensure that physicians remain surgery-prone. Ironically, physicians often unnecessarily remove ovaries during hysterectomies, causing infertility. Women and couples then seek help through reproductive technologies. This becomes a vicious cycle. Too many people have become dependent on the medical system to make their dreams a reality.

* * *

There is a bumper sticker which reads "If you can't trust me with a choice, how can you trust me with a child?" If women cannot make good decisions regarding prenatal health, then why are they given such enormous decision-making responsibility after a child is born? How can women make such good parents but lack such capacities when they are parents-to-be?

Early in my pregnancy I was offered the opportunity to have a maternal serum screening, which includes a blood test to determine whether the fetus is at risk for several birth defects. I am considered an "at risk" patient because I am over thirty-five years old. The test presents no risk to the fetus or the mother (except from a blood draw) but has a high rate of false positives. If it is positive, additional tests are recommended, including an ultrasound and/or amniocentesis. Amniocentesis carries its own risks: the fetus may be injured by it. I chose not to have the maternal serum screening. Although a negative result might have been reassuring, a positive one might have made me so nervous that my baby could have been adversely affected simply by my anxiety. I could have tried to allay the anxiety through further testing, but I did not want to risk injuring the baby and was particularly leery of amniocentesis.

I am glad that the serum test is available and that I had the choice to determine what was best for my child and myself. I know what I am capable of handling and am fairly well versed in reproductive issues. But what if that test had been mandatory, or what if certain subsequent actions were mandatory in the case of a positive result? Each case is so highly individualized that no edict should deprive women of their choices. No legislation forces women to breast-feed or to buy safe cribs; none should regulate important reproductive decisions.

Much of this book has focused on the need for regulation to assure that reproductive rights are upheld. This should not be misconstrued. Women do not need any more regulation over their reproductive lives, or any further diminution of their autonomy. Rather, the institutions that have gained control over women's reproductive rights need to be forced either to relinquish it or to set standards that minimize hazard and prohibit discrimination. Leaving industries and businesses, including the business of medicine, to regulate themselves has proven disastrous for women.

In a just world, devoid of sexism, heterosexism, racism, and capitalist greed, government regulation would be unnecessary. In an imperfect world such as our own, regulations can at least restrain abuse and come to the aid of its victims. Those who are discriminated against would at least have a legal recourse. However, protective regulation is on a continuum with paternalism, and it is easy to cross the fine line. Regulation that touches on reproductive issues and rights should originate from, and be developed and supervised by, individuals who are committed to the autonomy of women.

This book is a call to action. Organized advocates for women's rights, such as the National Organization for Women (NOW), the National Abortion Rights Action League (NARAL), the Feminist Majority Foundation, and the National Women's Health Network provide a focus for work toward true gender equality. But powerful forces are arrayed against them, intentionally or unintentionally opposing their goals. These range from antichoice groups to certain sectors of business and industry to the paternalistic tradition in law and government. Although many individuals and organizations seem to believe that they have a stake in controlling the reproductive rights of women, no one seems willing to take responsibility for any of the outcomes. How many, for example, of the thousands and thousands of Americans who do not believe a woman should have the right to choose abortion are prepared to adopt her unwanted children? The consequences of controlling a woman's reproductive choices fall overwhelmingly on the woman herself.

One purpose of this book is to provide readers with an opportunity to consider these issues as well as the ethical, medical, and legal rationales that underlie current practices. A broader and deeper public awareness of the issues will naturally bring to the fore advocates for women's health and reproductive rights who are better equipped to take on leadership roles. To paraphrase a quote that has often been attributed to Margaret Mead, "Never doubt that a small group of thoughtful, committed citizens can change the world. Indeed, it is the only thing that ever has."